Praise for
Money Loves . . .

'This book will help you to break the cycle and
come home to your innate abundance, so you can
live a life beyond your wildest dreams.'

REBECCA CAMPBELL, BEST-SELLING AUTHOR OF
YOUR SOUL HAD A DREAM, YOUR LIFE IS IT

'Farah is a bold, heartfelt new voice. Money Loves Me *is
a tender yet daring invitation to unearth the roots of our
relationship with money, drench our fears and wounds in
healing light, and love ourselves back to Wholeness. I could feel
Farah's deep soul wisdom permeating through each page.'*

SOPHIE BASHFORD, BEST-SELLING AUTHOR OF
YOU ARE A GODDESS

'Money Loves Me – right from the title, Farah announces the
arrival of a book which is radical in its refusal to conform to
the far too common discomfort with money. Farah's debut
book is a beautiful and unapologetic declaration of money as
divine energy – and our right to dance with it. In a writing
style that is both accessible and poetic, she chops through
narratives and hierarchies to reframe money and transform
our relationship with it into unconditional worthiness.
About so much more than anything material, this book is
a treasure with the potential to create powerful shifts in
how we experience money and how we love ourselves.'

JESSICA HUIE MBE, AUTHOR OF *PURPOSE*

MONEY

LOVES

ME

MONEY LOVES ME

The Spiritual Guide to Manifesting Abundance

FARAH ORTHS

HAY HOUSE

Carlsbad, California • New York City
London • Sydney • New Delhi

Published in the United States by: Hay House LLC, www.hayhouse.com® • P.O. Box 5100, Carlsbad, CA, 92018-5100

The information given in this book should not be treated as a substitute for professional medical advice; always consult a medical practitioner. Any use of information in this book is at the reader's discretion and risk. Neither the author nor the publisher can be held responsible for any loss, claim or damage arising out of the use, or misuse, of the suggestions made, the failure to take medical advice or for any material on third-party websites.

A catalogue record for this book is available from the British Library.

Tradepaper ISBN: 978-1-4019-7892-1
E-book ISBN: 978-1-83782-285-0
Audiobook ISBN: 978-1-83782-286-7

10 9 8 7 6 5 4 3 2 1

Printed in the United States of America

This product uses responsibly sourced papers, including recycled materials and materials from other controlled sources.

The authorized representative in the EU for product safety and compliance is Penguin Random House Ireland, Morrison Chambers, 32 Nassau Street, Dublin D02 YH68, Ireland. https://eu-contact.penguin.ie

I dedicate this book to my Pakistani nani (grandmother) in spirit, who gifted me a connection to unconditional divine love that I carry with me and offer to you in this book.

She always told me I would be an author, and here I am.

I love you. Thank you.

CONTENTS

OPENING WORDS

Before anything else, I want to extend a permission slip to those of you who may need it. I'm someone who appreciates a permission slip at the beginning of any program, journey, or container I enter into, so if you're like me, here is yours…

On this journey I invite you to take only what resonates. This book isn't here to convince you of anything. It isn't here to state, 'This is the only way!', it isn't here to say, 'You *have* to do x in order to get y and z.' This book is a humble offering from my heart to yours. What you do with it is fully *your* choice.

If anything I say or invite you to do doesn't feel good for your being or body, or supportive to you, remember that you are a powerful sovereign being and your intuition knows what's best for you – above *any* other person or teacher. Always. So, please don't pedestalize these teachings or force yourself into anything that doesn't feel expansive for you!

I trust you to navigate this book the way *you* want to. I trust your body's pace and timing. If that means reading a little at a time, if that means only reading one chapter and knowing that was the medicine for you, if that means putting the book down and integrating the teachings for months, if that means not doing all the exercises, it is sacred and welcome! Journey through this book *your* way. It's always the best way.

I also encourage you to add in your own wisdom and practices, if any come through for you.

And I wish you so much love on this journey.

Words

My teachings aren't associated with any organized religion or specific spiritual lineage, and neither are the words that I use. Words such as 'Divine,' 'Spirit,' 'Source,' 'God,' 'Creator,' and 'Creatrix' aren't used in the classically theistic way. I use these terms interchangeably to describe the source of unconditional love that I believe everything is birthed from. I actively encourage you to swap these words, if necessary, for ones that feel true and aligned with you and your life.

WELCOMING
ALL OF YOU

Welcome. When you hear the word 'welcome,' breathe it in. Just as you would when getting out into nature and smelling the crisp air – taking it all in, tasting it.

Tasting it as if it's the first time you've truly felt what the word 'welcome' means.

Take a moment and feel each cell within you hearing this word and relaxing into this moment as it realizes it's safe to be here.

Breathe in.

Breathe out.

The truth is, you *are* welcome here.

Truly.

My prayer is that as you open this book again and again, you feel you're opening the doors of the coziest place you can imagine, being ushered inside, out of the harsh cold winds of life, and nestling into the depths of warmth and love. The pages of this book are so happy to have you here reading them. They've been waiting for you to go on this journey into the heart of money, and ultimately into the heart of who you are – *a deeply and infinitely abundant soul, learning how to embody that in your human self.*

All of you – energetically, physically, and spiritually – is invited into this experience.

Bringing all of yourself is the only way forward when you are working with the frequency of money – bringing all the parts of yourself that have been hurting, in fear, in survival around abundance, and equally the soul that has been asking you to embody your wholeness, your infinite power, and the radical abundance you hold. You will meet these parts as you traverse the landscapes money has shaped, observing and integrating until your wholeness is realized and embodied, and a felt sense of this truth restored.

This is a journey of radical and immense love.

The only way anything is healed is through deep love. You will learn how loved you are, and that money is a wise spirit that is here to embrace you and guide you with its wisdom. It holds the map to your freedom, because it can mirror your deepest shadows and guide you to liberation precisely and clearly.

Some of you may have grown up with a lot of money, some may have debt, some may have money flowing into your bank accounts and yet feel disconnected from it, and some may simply be desiring a deeper spiritual connection to how money fits into your life. Others may have just felt the pull of this book and be opening to the mystery of why you are reading this as you go along. However you came to be here, *welcome.* You are in the right place, at the perfect time. The Spirit of Money has chosen this time to reveal itself to you and take you on a powerful journey back into the arms of the Divine. It's no coincidence that you're reading this book now. I know that your being is about to reveal its abundance to you.

So, whatever your story, know it's time to become *more* of who you came here to be.

I've seen so many teachers of 'money mindset' teach in a way that made me feel I had to be someone else before I could even begin to heal my relationship with money. They offered money healing that was all about the numbers, the income you could hit like it was a target, and how to blast through your limiting beliefs as if it was a race to a glitzy lifestyle…

This book isn't like that. This is a journey with soul, with heart. No glitziness, no prescribed lifestyle, just your heart's dream guiding you into the heart of money so that *your* most authentic life can be birthed and *your* highest vision can become your waking reality. Organically. Your way.

For most of my life I genuinely believed, with my whole being, that I would always be rubbish with money. *I didn't believe that who I was was compatible with money.* As a mixed-race brown girl in England, I was convinced that money was for others, not for me.

Over the years, I read books about money, consumed and saved countless social media reels and posts about it, and tried to figure it all out. But there was a patriarchal and capitalistic flavor to most money-mindset books that left me feeling that they weren't written for someone like me – someone on the spiritual path, devoted to a life in the arms of the Divine. And what I didn't see was anybody speaking about the very real scared human that pops up when it comes to money healing. I didn't hear anyone say, 'It's okay if you're frightened. It's okay if you don't believe you can heal this. It's okay if your mind says all sorts of things about you and money. It doesn't always tell the truth, but it's allowed to speak.'

For a lot of my life, what my mind told me was that money hated me. I felt sick and anxious and so ashamed whenever I thought of it. I thought there was something inherently flawed within me that somehow made it impossible for money to love me.

Since I've been holding money-healing courses and spaces, I've heard countless people express their version of the same thing. 'I'm scared my money stuff is just *too big* and *too deep* to heal.' 'I've tried all the affirmations and courses and nothing changes!'

If you, too, have an inner voice echoing that sentiment, I want to speak to that part of you – the part that wants to put this book down or switch off.

Let's start this journey together by turning to that part and saying:

Hi! I see you. It's not a problem that you're here. It's not a problem that you're scared of money healing or feel it won't work. You get to sit at this table. And we're going to let the Spirit of Money take us on a journey, no matter what you say. You don't have to disappear for me to have a very powerful experience with this book. You don't have to go anywhere for me to remember how powerful I am and how much love is waiting for me in my relationship with abundance.

What a relief that you get to bring *all* of yourself on this journey – your resistance, your doubt, your cynicism. I encourage you to bring them all along. Extend a hand to your excitement, too. Your hope. Your tiredness. Your willingness. Your dreams. Bring the radical truth of who you are. The mystery of your becoming. There are seats at the table for all those parts.

Because guess what? I have *all* those parts too. I continue to be in a living relationship with money that ebbs and flows because it is alive, as we all are, and this means I also still have fear and doubt and excitement and tiredness and ancestral patterns and blocks, *and* power. It *all* still journeys with me. And it always will!

I dare you to bring it all along, too. There's not one human emotion, thought, or belief that isn't welcome here, that is 'too much' or 'not enough.' You don't have to pretend here. The more truthful you allow yourself to be, the more specifically these words will touch you and the deeper the healing will be. We can only heal what we reveal.

This is a money-healing book for the real human. There's no bypassing here, no 'thinking your way into money.' This is a book that was written for your heart, with my love.

It will never be for those who aspire to be the 'perfect' spiritual person who is only love and light. It's for the perfectly imperfect, still learning, vulnerable, and courageous one who wants their relationship to money to feel so much spiritually richer than it has up to now. It's for you. For me. For us.

It's for the person with conflicting beliefs, the one who thinks they are a being of infinite light but also has a frightened child within them, the one who sometimes says the wrong things, the one who wants to throw a tantrum about why money has been the way it has in their life, the one who knows they're destined for big things and yet is afraid to receive goodness in life, the one who tries so hard yet keeps finding patterns of scarcity repeating... I've been there. I still am there at times. I am you and you are me!

Because isn't that what we *all* really are? Aren't we all unavoidably human, underneath the facades? We need a money-healing map that's made for the very real human.

What we will come to see is that money has never been asking us to be anything other than human. That it wants all of us. And the unconditional love that it offers us may be a revolution that reaches far beyond our relationship with money. And maybe, just maybe, money is here for a much bigger purpose in our lives than we could ever have imagined.

A Loving Guide

It's important that you know that this book is here as a loving guide. It's actually a love story – *your love story with money*. And, just like falling in love with a person, the love only really begins when we reveal the messy and imperfect yet perfect human that we are and tentatively, bashfully, and sometimes shakily ask, 'Do you still love me? Even after seeing all of that?'

This is the book to let love into those places... so being messy is kinda the *whole* point. And the real question is:

Are you ready to
fall in love and be loved?

To go on this journey is to reach into the corners of your being, the shadows, the less visited places within you, and shine a light to reveal what wants to be cleared and brought into love again.

I know that even approaching the topic of money can feel triggering and scary. I get this to my core. We aren't here to bypass any of that. But it's safe to work with money. It's safe to open yourself up to the loving spirit within money.

Not only is it safe, but your soul chose to enter this world at a time when money existed. It's so very easy to say, 'I wish money didn't exist!' but that is to deny the age that we live in. Your soul chose to live in a society with money as a form of exchange, and your soul picked up this book, so I ask you to trust your soul's timing and purpose: to enable you to start to understand what money really is, so you can live more fully, with deeper ease, in this lifetime.

How you engage with this book determines how you experience it. You want to be creating as much evidence as you can for your body that money is safe, money is kind, and money wants to love you and be with you, and that there is nothing to fear. That money is an energy you can speak to often, like a friend, and communicate with, emotionally and spiritually.

Practically, I invite you to see this book as one you're excited to dive into. The more you can create a really cozy, relaxing atmosphere around reading it, the better. See it as like picking up your fave magical witchy fiction book! (That's what I like anyway... feel free to insert your own favorite here.)

You see, your nervous system needs physical-world evidence that money is safe – safe to speak about, to receive, to desire, to engage with, to exist with. This book that you're holding in your hands right now is a great piece of evidence to start with.

See the Words

I chose the title of this book intentionally, as a loving spell and mantra. It holds *so* much power in healing your relationship with money that I suggest you display the book in your bedroom or somewhere else where you can *see* those words every day and let the magic of subconscious suggestion do its thing for you.

When you reach for your book, see yourself picking up a piece of your heart. Receiving a hug from the Divine. And then settle down to enjoy reading it. If you can make a nourishing warm drink a part of your reading ritual and get really comfortable, your body will start to slowly create a new pathway that says, 'Money is an energy I am at peace with and look forward to being with.' This will release a lot of resistance in your field and allow your innate money magnetism to flow.

Be Kind to Yourself

To go on this journey is to reach into the corners of your being, the shadows, the less visited places within you, and shine a light to reveal what wants to be cleared and brought into love again. It is to clear the cobwebs, reclaim the abandoned parts of your being, and regain the power waiting in those forgotten places within. It is a journey home.

Like any deep spiritual and emotional initiation, it may be uncomfortable at times. I invite you to remember that every trigger that arises is only asking to be dissolved into love. Any 'shadow' isn't there to attack you or bring you down, but to ask you to rise up and hold that part of yourself that has been hurt by life with so much love and devotion that its sting melts away and you sink into deeper softness.

Learning the Language of Money

There is an art to understanding the Spirit of Money and its language. It is a felt sense that will develop with time. Sometimes the Spirit of Money will invite you into deeper love by showing you through your emotions how much shame you still hold in your body. This isn't to keep you there, but to allow you to sit with the shame until it's no longer shame, but acceptance. We will journey with this later on in greater detail.

Sometimes the Spirit of Money will bring up all the fearful thoughts and scarcity about money that have been sitting in your body your whole life, or even further back in your lineage. Again, this isn't to torture you, but to show you how much energy has been going into these patterns of survival and to ask you whether you are ready to put them down and step into ease for yourself and your lineage.

Similarly, parts of you may show up and ask you to put down the book and stop the inner inquiry simply because your nervous system is wired to stay in what is known. Anything that is known is 'safe' to the nervous system, even if it's actually really unhelpful for your life and liberation. So, your nervous system will want to keep you in your comfort zone because it believes this is the only way you will survive. Your nervous system really, really cares about you. Its only job is to keep you alive and well.

Here's the thing, though – every single dream, yearning, soul knowing of how big and beautiful a life you are meant for is on a nervous-system level classed as 'unknown.' Yet on a soul level, the life you hope for *is* so *known and safe*. It's *already* yours – your nervous system just has to catch up with this fact. So remember that it's not just safe but *vital* for you to leave your comfort zone.

Start now, moving step by step through this book, and finally create a new zone where you truly thrive instead of just survive.

If you find yourself in emotional pain or facing triggers and discomfort as you shed old patterns on this journey and expand beyond your comfort zone, I invite you to celebrate those times, even just for a moment. Trust that you are moving forward. The art of seeing beneath a trigger is the art of trusting the divine intelligence in your body and the love for your expansion that it operates through.

Also, know these codes are working on a deeper level. By 'codes,' I mean teachings that hold a certain vibration and frequency that can be used to rewrite your internal world. These codes have a frequency that can shift your energy field without it needing to be on the conscious level. So when facing the mirrors and discomfort that can arise during times of shifting your frequency and field toward money, know that this is exactly when the denser parts of you are being liberated into the light. See it as a victory that what was once so hidden that you couldn't even see it has chosen to come out of the shadows, and know that when it does this, it's a pattern that's already on its way out.

You are witnessing a death that is necessary for the rebirth you have been praying for.

It's all happening for you. It's all for your healing.

It's part of a rebirth of your relationship to life itself.

Take off the well-worn shoes of who you have
been and walk barefoot on this journey as you
remember who you were before you settled for less.

Place a hand on your heart and read this welcome prayer out loud, breathing in each line and receiving a deep embrace from this book:

Radical Welcome Prayer

I welcome all parts of myself, seen and unseen, into this journey.

I welcome all of my ancestors, seen and unseen, into this journey.

I welcome all versions of myself, seen and unseen, into this journey.

I invite all loving guides of this world and beyond to gather around me and usher me forward with ease and grace.

I relax my body and soul and let the Spirit Guide of Money show me the way.

I recognize the sacred intelligence of triggers and remember that they only ever desire to bring me home into love.

I release all harshness and criticism of myself and choose the path of softness as my default on this path into my soul.

I allow this book to bring me into a deeper embrace of myself and life itself.

I allow the Spirit of Money to show me how big I came here to be.

And I remember that I am the ancestor I have been waiting for and the power I have been praying for.

I do not need to settle for less any longer.

This ends with me. And this starts with me.

I say 'yes' to the most beautiful spiritual connection between me and money.

I come home to my divine abundance, breath by breath, line by line of this book.

And so it is.

———————————

CHAPTER 1

YOUR HUMANNESS IS MAGNETIC

'This being human is a guest house.
Each morning a new arrival...

A joy, a depression... some momentary awareness
comes as an unexpected visitor...

Meet them at the door... and invite them in.

Be grateful for whoever comes,
because each has been sent
as a guide from beyond.'

RUMI

Breathe in...

Breathe out...

I have yet to meet someone who hasn't had a deeply painful part of this human life, something they hold shame around, something they battle with in secret. Many people in the spiritual community call this our 'darkness.' There are so many interpretations of what darkness is, and often subconscious shaming of it. So I want to share what I mean by the term and illuminate how the way you interact with your own perceived darkness ends up shaping the way you interact with money.

You see, darkness is simply a part of our human experience that we have decided isn't worthy of existing.

So we cloak it in fear and cast it to the back of our minds, hoping it will somehow disappear. But it's really this *casting away* process, this rejection, that ultimately creates the darkness. Everything becomes dark if we starve it of light and starve it of love, yet no part of us is truly 'dark.' The 'dark' pieces are just pieces of us that need love.

Take the universe, for example – all the dark matter, the space, the void. We could approach this with fear, meaning it is suddenly translated into the scary unknown, danger, a threat, something to ignore, avoid, or suppress, *or* we could approach it with wonder. Instead of seeing it as empty and scary, we could see it as full of endless possibility.

> *When we love the 'dark,' we don't experience*
> *it as negative anymore, we experience it as*
> *fertile, complex, rich, intriguing, inviting.*

We begin to understand it, and how it fits into the greater picture of our lives, in new and important ways.

My Journey with 'Darkness'

From the youngest age, I was a deep feeler and thinker... I would sit in the back of the car on journeys home, looking up at the stars, crying over the nature of our existence, and wondering what happened to us when we passed. I was wondering what the meaning of life was when I was only nine years old. I had a hyperawareness and sensitivity that made me feel that I was seeing the world so differently from everyone else.

I now know that's a gift. At the age of 12, however, I began to journey into my own 'darkness,' a part of my human experience that would, over a decade later, radically transform my life.

But first, it had to break me open and *undo who I thought I was.*

I experienced what I now know to be called 'intrusive thoughts' and Pure OCD, which is a type of obsessive-compulsive disorder focused on the monitoring of thoughts. At the time, I had no words for what was happening.

Having intrusive thoughts is an isolating and debilitating experience that centers around having disturbing or unwanted thoughts pop into your mind at the most unpredictable moments. Then with Pure OCD, you become obsessive about them out of fear. It feels like your mind is on some serious fear steroids and is trying to find anything that confirms there's something deeply wrong with you or the present moment.

I would experience out-of-the-blue thoughts like *What if I'm capable of murder?* or *What if the car that's coming toward me mounts the curb and I die?* or even unwanted sexual scenarios.

For years, my most recurrent belief about myself was that there really was something deeply wrong with me and that I was unfixable. In the days when I believed in the classic man-in-the-sky kinda God, I remember thinking that God had somehow created everyone else to function well, but had messed up with me, leaving me with the strangest mind on Earth.

The thoughts were so scary, embarrassing, and disturbing that I couldn't ever utter them out loud to anybody, because I thought they'd lock me away if they knew.

It was a heartbreaking case of mistaken identity – for years, I believed that I *was* my thoughts, and therefore *I* was disturbed and dangerous.

My only coping mechanism was to push the thoughts away, having mental battles to try and resist them, which in the end only made them more persistent, and I started to have panic attacks regularly, which grew into a bout of depression in my early twenties. It felt as if someone was torturing me from within my own mind. I felt trapped and miserable. I couldn't go outside for help, and I had nowhere safe to go within. I remember thinking that I didn't want to live anymore, if this was the mind that I had to live with for the rest of my life...

While many people look back at their teen and young adult years with a sweet nostalgia and a fondness for that time of their lives, I look back with pain in my heart because of what that young Farah went through.

Finding the Heart's Balm

I'm sharing what I went through because there's a pulsing golden thread that leads all the way from that time to this moment now, when I'm sharing this book with you: held by life and the Divine, with a community of truly incredible people in my life and the opportunity to thrive through my soul work of teaching and guiding spiritual people to heal their relationship with money – and ultimately their relationship with their inescapable and holy humanness. I know I am lovable, I know I am more loved by the Divine than I could ever have dreamed possible, and when an intrusive thought pops up, I'm able to simply witness it arising, because I know who I really am *and* I have accepted my humanness. Being human is a journey I will always be on in this lifetime, there's no escaping it. We *all* have our human 'stuff.' There is no 'finish line' with human healing. Knowing this can relax you like nothing else!

The truth is that the intrusive thoughts were my awakening. Without them, I might never have been called to look within and find out who I really was.

I had been initiated, earlier than most, into the soul-searching journey of understanding what people all over the world go on meditation retreats, pilgrimages, psychedelic journeys, and deep inner inquiry to find: what and who we really are. Underneath all the noise. All the thoughts. All that society conditions us to believe. And how we make peace with what we discover within.

I had to learn not to resist my humanness and the monkey mind that we all have. The weird thoughts that we all have at times. The pain that we all face. Like many, I tried rejecting those parts of myself for nearly a decade, only to end up in a worse place than where I started.

So, through this involuntary experiment, I slowly learned the only thing that made sense and brought me into peace, that brought me back to the moment, every single time, and that gave me some relief from the darkness I felt: I learned how to truly embody unconditional love for myself. And my practice was to do so dozens of times a day, every time an intrusive thought arose.

The only choice I had that helped was to take a deep breath and actively turn toward the thoughts that I wanted to run from.

The only words that offered refuge every time were: 'It's okay that you are here.'

I had to practice knowing that I was lovable even with all the things I thought made me totally unlovable, every single day for years. Looking back, I laugh and say the universe put me in unofficial monk training.

To this day, I find that phrase, 'It's okay that you are here,' one of the most soothing and instantly calming sentences we can offer our emotions and thoughts. All the fight within gives up, all the resistance melts, and we realize the monster we thought we were fighting just wants to sit at the table with us, without being rejected or 'fixed.'

With a *lot* of practice, I started to birth a loving internal world for myself, a place that had cushions and seats at the table for *all* the parts of myself, a world that wasn't naive about the humanness that all of us have to traverse. I came to the understanding that our humanness doesn't make us weak or 'less than' and doesn't define us.

It's still a *practice* to this very day.

As I moved through my twenties, I started to see that most of us feel there's something wrong with us and that we're all suffering from not understanding that imperfection is *normal* and *expected* when you're human.

We're here on this human journey to turn toward the most shamed 'dark' parts of us and offer the balm of radical acceptance.

It's the only way forward. For it's also how we learn to love in the same way. *Unconditionally.*

I know if you're reading this book you'll have your own version of the darkness journey that was so painful that it called you to your healing journey, or perhaps you're in the middle of an unraveling through pain right now.

But the invisible invitation to venture into the heart of our pain is a loving awakening. A healing. A returning to the home of our soul. So, when we avoid the pain and the darkness, we also miss out on the gift that is being offered to us.

High Vibe or Avoidance?

There is purpose in our pain. And yet, early on in my spiritual awakening journey, I saw something that surprised me immensely: the number of 'spiritual' people who wanted to do anything *but* sit with their pain. There was a tendency to cast the pain to the pavement, as if it were a useless dirty thing that would only hold you back... A whole part of the community and manifestation 'industry' was actively committed to teaching people to bypass their pain as if it wasn't sacred.

I had already done many years of therapy and ancestral healing by this point, so I had a certain understanding of how I best navigated myself as a human, and I'd taken a lot of time to stop shaming the humanness that we all experience – the messy emotions, the triggers, the parts of us that wobble (emotionally and physically). In the world of manifestation, however, I was constantly being told that the best way to manifest the life I wanted was simply to be 'high-vibe.'

Everywhere I looked I was being told that the higher your frequency and emotions, the more you would manifest beautiful things in your life... All that I had learned about loving whatever arose and welcoming all emotions and parts of ourselves as equally worthy was being challenged.

Now, before we go deeper, I want to be clear that I understand why that teaching is so widely shared and how beautiful it is to be able to choose to be grateful and in a state of ecstatic union with life! It's a part of my lived experience too. As an energy healer, I absolutely believe in the power of our frequency as a foundation for our life, *and* here's where I feel there's something missing, something we can add to that picture that allows our beings to take a big sigh of relief and allows us to be *all* that we are *and* deeply magnetic throughout all our moon phases.

When we're told that certain emotions are the ones to focus on and that they will bring us the money, the house, the life we dream of, we very quickly and subconsciously develop an inner emotional hierarchy, one that we hold others to by default.

When we think certain emotions are good and magnetic and others aren't good and reduce our magnetism, what happens when we feel sadness, fear, or grief? All these are expected, vital, and healthy expressions of being alive. They are innate to the cycles of every living being in this world. But when we feel them, we feel shame. We feel that something is wrong. That we shouldn't be feeling the way we are.

That way of understanding manifestation is based on *conditional* love.

This is when we are asked to go back to the Divine.

Feel into your connection with the Divine/Goddess/God/loving awareness/the universe right now, and ask yourself whether you believe this all-loving force, upon looking at you when you're crying in bed, for example, would ever say:

- 'She's not high-vibe enough to receive right now!'

- 'He's not in his power enough for beautiful things to happen for him.'

- 'They don't believe in miracles enough for us to send them one!'

Does that feel like something the unconditionally loving universe would do?

Whenever I ask people this question, they always have a strong sense that the Divine doesn't have these filters for us. Yet, collectively and individually, we act as if we do believe the Divine loves us based on what we *do* or think instead of simply our existence.

There's also *so* much evidence of people magnetizing and manifesting the most miraculous things when they don't have a clue about what manifestation is or what high-vibe even means! There are so many examples of people having incredible things happen for them in the midst of suffering, in the midst of a divorce, in the midst of grieving for someone. Where's the 'high vibe' in those situations?

There have been *so* many days when I've been tumbling in a wave of emotions, not feeling 'magnetic' at all, and yet while I've been in bed crying and doubting, money has been rolling into my bank account, unbeknown to me, from people joining my online course while I've just been letting myself be human.

Living through Unconditional Love

I invite you to rip down all the hierarchies and judgments of one emotion being better or more magnetic than another. I invite you to feel the radical acceptance of the Divine in every single part of you. I invite you to move from a system of conditional and volatile worthiness to *unconditional* and steady worth.

When we look deeper at the major religions of the world, we see that they often operate on the frequency of conditional love, even if their scriptures say something different. For example, if you do right by others, you will be 'rewarded,' but if you sin or don't pray or attend church or mosque, you will be punished and will have to repent and pray for forgiveness.

Have we as a spiritual community subconsciously let conditional love filter into our relationship with the Divine?

The liberating truth is that the universe always loves us.

The deepest truth is that we are being *unconditionally* loved every single moment of our lives. We are *unconditionally* aligned.

It was never the *universe* judging us, *it was us judging ourselves.* And this came about through our conditioning of what the Divine was and what the laws of manifestation were. It was the paradigm of believing parts of us were more lovable than others that formed this distortion. It was the striving to be 'perfect' – something no human is ever meant to achieve. So, it's time to let that paradigm dissolve now. It's time to let the perfectionist die. It's time to let the inner critic rest. It's time to be holy and human. Just as we all are. Are you in?

In every state. In every trigger. In every expression. Spirit won't blink. There is no off-switch to its love. There is no 'man in the sky' judging whether we are worthy, based on our emotions or frequency, or thoughts. We are continually loved, as though it's the easiest thing in the world.

In fact, I believe the Divine has never been 'up there,' it has always been 'right here,' and when we descend into our humanness, we find the sacred right there with us. We were birthed in this lifetime to be embodied humans, not to ascend or escape our humanness, as many spiritual seekers attempt to do.

The Divine lives in every single cell within us.
In every emotion that arises, there is divinity.

This one understanding may just change your life. It certainly changed mine. If you can access the feeling of unconditional love whenever you need to, everything opens up for you.

It's time to let the perfectionist die.

It's time to let the inner critic rest.

It's time to be holy and human.

Just as we all are.

If you step out of resistance to what is arising, you're able to be present, you're able to say what you need to, you're able to channel and create what is asking to come through.

Your life will become radically supported and so rich with compassion and grace because you never turn away from yourself or believe that the Divine has left you.

In this state, *ease* will finally find you, because you're no longer resisting the present moment. You're resting in the knowledge that the Divine is present in every experience and you're always held, always carried. From within.

When you yourself drop any judgment of where you are and rip out the hierarchy or scale of emotions, rip out the hierarchy or timeline of where you 'should be at,' internally or externally, you suddenly allow love to be with you right that second. Nothing may have changed on the outside, but everything has changed on the inside.

This rewiring is fundamental, because we can move into a state of feeling unconditionally loved by the Divine instead of conditionally loved.

The Divine is already here, loving every one of us every single day, every single moment, every single mood… we get to decide whether we let it in or not.

The Divine and Money

This unconditional love is the *foundation* that our lives can be built upon. Doing the energy work, choosing our frequency, and being devoted to clearing and moving density out of our field can only be healthy for us if we build it on a foundation of unconditional love. It is *this* that sets us up for the most liberating relationship with money too.

You see, divine loving consciousness lives within money, and money is a part of the divine fabric of this world. They are one and the same. So, just as the Divine wants you and loves you in every state of your being and your cycles, the Spirit of Money does too.

The deep love that the Divine has for you is
the exact same love that Money has for you.

What does it feel like to understand that Money wants *you* just as you are? Right now? That your humanness has never been a problem for Money, because it has never been a problem for the Divine?

In fact, Money sees your humanness as easy to love. I invite you to close your eyes and really let that in. Take a mental snapshot of how you're feeling right now – every ache, every open and tense part of you, every doubt and dream, every thought, every area of your life, and everything in between... Feel Money saying 'yes' to it all. So easily.

Feel Money saying, 'You're perfect just the way you are right now. There is no becoming that you ever have to do for me to want to be with you!'

This is a practice. Just as I had to practice day by day, thought by thought, to love whatever arose in my monkey mind, practice is needed to build an unconditionally loving relationship with Money.

Letting money love you is a journey. It's a daily decision. It will build over time into something you're able to access so quickly! Yet at the start, it may feel clunky. That's okay. Choose to let Money love you anyway. Let your nervous system start to feel safe in unconditional love, knowing it's what your soul has been guiding you into all along. It's returning to what you were born from.

So, yearning to heal your relationship with Money becomes a journey to meet the depths of unconditional love from the Divine. The Spirit of Money is here to deliver you into the love of the Divine.

If you allow it to be, every daily interaction with Money gets to be a place of opening to love. Every daily interaction with Money gets to be an opportunity to deepen your trust in the Divine. Every daily interaction with Money gets to be you recognizing your own unconditional worth and finally embracing the perfectly imperfect human you came here to be!

This is what the Spirit of Money is really here for.

Introducing Richuals

To conclude every chapter, you'll be offered a 'richual.' This is a short exercise, journal prompt, or journey that will help the chapter's words to sink in in a more embodied way. If it feels right for you, I highly recommend doing the richuals to integrate what has been shared in each chapter. You may want to keep a separate journal dedicated to this money-healing journey. You can also use the exercises as inspiration to do more journaling of your own and let them lead you further into money healing, guided by your intuition.

RICHUAL

✦ Write down all the emotions you've been conditioned to believe are 'blocking your magnetism.' All the times that you believe money cannot find you. When do you believe you aren't magnetic? For example, *When I'm feeling sad. When I'm not thinking 'high-vibe' thoughts. When I'm doubting that things will work out. When I'm not feeling confident. When I'm in my sweatpants watching TV.*

✦ Let this reveal to you the conditional love that you may be holding for yourself and projecting onto the Divine's love for you. Once you can clearly witness all the things you think you have to change *before* Money can truly love you, start to see all those things as *perfectly easy* to love in Spirit's eyes and in Money's eyes.

✦ Go through the list and feel the Spirit of Money not even blink, because you are *so beyond* lovable that Money wants to be with you all the time, including in the exact states of being you wrote down.

✦ Write down next to each emotion and state: 'It's easy for Money to love me when I am like this!' Each and every one.

Soul Affirmation

'There has never been a more perfect time for money to flow to me than right now. Right here. Just the way I am.'

CHAPTER 2

WHO IS MONEY
TO YOU?

*'We cannot heal what we
have not grieved.'*

Breathe in...

Breathe out...

One of the most profound healings I have ever gone through has been in my relationship to the lands of England... As a Pakistani–German bi-racial brown girl who only moved to England at the age of seven, with a thick German accent, I didn't have any sense of belonging in the UK until I was 28 years old.

All that time, the history of Britain and its colonial Empire, in the world and in the countries my lineage ran through, meant that I felt deep grief and anger toward these lands. It was all I could feel whenever I thought of 'Great' Britain.

I truly didn't know where I belonged. I remember a therapist asking me, 'Where on this Earth do you feel safe?' and my answer being, 'In space, away from this planet.' I had never felt true safety here. And I couldn't see a future where I would want to be in England. I felt too triggered by it.

There was so much anger inside of me that I didn't know what to do with it or where to place it. And so, in my twenties, I traveled, feeling more at home in other countries than I ever had in England.

Looking back, in many ways, my relationship with England mirrored many people's relationship with money – an energetic collection of trauma, conditioning, and stories blocking access to the real heart.

It wasn't until the age of 28, when I was training to hold Sacred Drum Circles in a beautiful yurt with a roaring fire in the depths of winter in rural Northumberland, while it snowed heavily around us, that everything changed.

Every day we were invited to call in the land to hold us and journey with us. Being the only woman of color on the training, I knew I was having a very different experience of this than the rest of the women. With every day that passed, my anger and disconnection from the land that everyone around me so effortlessly connected to and loved grew louder and louder, until I shared with the group of English sisters that I *didn't* feel the land loving me, I *didn't* feel the land holding me... In fact, all I felt when I connected to the land was *pain*.

Whether it was the result of the trauma of the racism experienced by me and my family, the ancestral imprint of skinheads holding knives to the throat of my mum, a child at the time, in the 70s, or the way I was bullied because of my accent, or being told my mum was a terrorist, or the colonial history of these lands, I couldn't find the loving spirit in the land.

Given that my spiritual path was to find and communicate with the loving spirit in everything, I felt shame and frustration over this. It felt like my roots just couldn't root as they were meant to.

As I expressed this through sobs, letting the grief pour out of me, the space holder, Melonie said she felt called to ask the circle of women to drum for me and give me the welcome I should have had when I arrived in England. She asked if that felt right for me, and I didn't expect much to come of it, so I said, 'Yes, why not?'

I sat in the middle of the circle, closed my eyes, and took myself back to a memory I had of being on the playground all alone, not fully knowing the language and feeling a cold and vast sense of loneliness. No friends or warm faces around me. A chill in the air.

It felt like I was right back there again.

And then the women started to drum...

They whispered, sang, and spoke welcoming words and gave soothing gifts of love to me, while keeping the steady beat of Mother Earth all around me.

They radiated joy that I had arrived in England, as if I was what they had all been eagerly anticipating, instead of something they could just about tolerate.

The 'foreigner' and 'immigrant' feeling started to melt slightly. Where I had felt so 'other,' I started to feel a kinship with the English people.

And slowly, subtly, the loving faces of the women were appearing in the playground with me, all around me. They were so happy that my soul had decided to live in England. I was a gift they were welcoming.

Through the release of the grief, through the witnessing of the rage and deep hurt and lack of connection... and then the immense sincere and loving welcome from those women, I finally understood something: I had spent my life interacting with the trauma layer of England, a layer that we project all of our experiences onto until the land itself seems disfigured, a mirror of our own internal world. But the truth was that the core of the lands – the *heart* of England's lands – had always existed. I hadn't been able to feel it. But it had been there, holding me, all along...

All of a sudden I realized that it was in *England* that I'd had the spiritual awakening that had brought me home to my core, it was in *England* that Spirit had communicated with me for many years, keeping me tethered to love and offering me my spiritual awakening, it was in *England* that magic had poured through me and created through me.

It had all happened in England. The land that I felt hated me.

Suddenly I understood that my roots could never have sunk into the layer of trauma I thought was England before. But now they could sink into the heart of the land... I could make a connection I couldn't have understood before.

Since then, I haven't needed to run away anymore. Since that deep release and connection to the true heart of these lands, since being welcomed and being witnessed in my grief, I have felt utterly in love with England, *something I never thought I would experience in my lifetime.*

This story mirrors the experience of money that many have.

They spend a lifetime interacting through their trauma body with a version of money that isn't the real heart of it. They can't imagine a beautiful relationship with it because they've been plugging into one frequency, *one layer,* of it, the layer that holds all the trauma – their family's trauma, their own, society's trauma with money... all of it.

We want to grow the seeds of a new identity and relationship with money by planting them in the heart of money, not the layer that holds the trauma. But to get to the heart, the trauma has to be acknowledged, witnessed, and given space to exist with unwavering compassion. The trauma has to speak, has to be heard.

It isn't until the grief and anger have been felt that there is hope for a new future.

Facing the trauma, the grief, and letting it come out is what we often resist the most – our instincts are to keep it in, hold it tighter and tighter, swallow it, force it down deeper and deeper, and yet it's acknowledging the grieving heart that frees a miraculously clear space within.

The Courage to Grieve

My sense is that if you're reading this book, if it has found its way into your hands or you've picked it up yourself, you are truly and utterly *courageous* – far beyond what you may know yourself to be. Your hand clicking 'buy' or reaching out for this book on the shelf was your deeper knowing moving you closer to the most expansive and abundant way of relating to life. And this kind of healing – any kind of healing – takes an immense amount of courage.

When we go on the journey of healing, we have to leave big chunks of ourselves behind – ancestral patterns, inner safety coping mechanisms, societal expectations, and ways of relating to ourselves. Healing is to be in constant relationship with death and rebirth. Aligning ourselves with a new frequency means an old frequency dies. Every time we choose a new thought pattern, a comforting and well-worn thought pattern ceases to exist. *We are shedding skins from the inside out.*

Yet while on the healing journey, we rarely recognize our courage. So often we see ourselves as broken or weak for having things to heal 'from.' We all have things to heal 'from.' I haven't met a single human who doesn't. Imperfect humans have raised imperfect humans who have raised imperfect humans, who have affected one another.

Equally, I've met extremely brave humans listening to the call of their wholeness instead of their 'brokenness.' Choosing to open bravely to life instead of staying shut down, small, and closed. Listening to the call of the divine right of abundance instead of a society or family system that accepts less. Looking to expand their lineage instead of settling, like the generations before.

Before we get to the liberated *high*, though, we must face what the internal deaths bring up. And here's where courage really comes in...

The Truth of the Moment

In every ceremony I hold, both personally and publicly, and in every circle I facilitate, the first rite of passage is a *welcoming practice*. This is a permission slip to welcome the *truth* of the moment the person finds themselves in.

Searing honesty is needed for this stage. As is shedding all expectations of themselves and giving words to the truth of their emotions, their state of mind, and the sensations in their body – without filter or refrain. This is what I call looking into the Mirror of Truth.

Let this chapter be a version of that mirror. It will show you energies and stories picked up long ago about money. And I mean a *long* time ago.

Feel the Weight to Free It

We all arrived in this world with energetic stories about money, about power and pain, about work, about self-worth, and about what's possible for 'people like us' – stories from our parents and ancestors that have been woven into our DNA, which the well-researched field of epigenetics can confirm.

We can picture this as babies coming into this world with invisible bags attached to their little bodies. With those airport tags that say: 'Heavy.'

As we grow, these bags of information about money grow with us. So, how can we expect ourselves to just magically feel free and liberated?! First we must look into the bags that we have been carrying.

This is your chance to look into those bags, open that storybook, see and feel what's there, and then – and *only* then – rewrite the pages.

When we come into close contact with money, we're interacting with a web of our life's experiences with money. Money has had layers and layers of projection and traumatic experiences and desires and hopes placed upon it until its real essence has been buried under a pile of 'clothes that don't fit.'

Unsurprisingly, triggers arise before we have even had a chance to catch our breath – at the checkout, when we log into our banking apps, or think about traveling or saving up for a house... Old patterns of scarcity or survival come up, ways to control, plan, save... all arise subconsciously.

Or maybe the trauma shows up in the guise of a fear of dreaming of more for ourselves – a familiar tightness in our body, a sensation of anxiety, or maybe a numbness.

This energetic web of what money represents often feels like a mountain to 'get over,' doesn't it? No wonder so many of us try and avoid money healing for so long! Yet in the meantime, life goes on, patterns get more entrenched, and we end up feeling trapped by the identities we have formed about who we are with money. Which ends up affecting so much of our lives.

Let's open the space for a different approach to this money mountain... Stop and think for a moment. What if you don't need to 'climb' the mountain?

What if there's no sense of 'conquering' needed here?

What if you don't need to untangle the whole web with a view to 'fixing' something?

What if there's nothing to even run away from here?

What if... you just need to *feel* the mountain? Every inch. Every crack. Every sharp edge, every hard place, every ravine, every shadow.

What if you're being given an opportunity to become lovingly intimate with the mountain – with the parts of you that have been trying to communicate with you for a long time?

Breathe into the fire of longing

that asks you to believe in

more for yourself.

Breathe into your very nature –

the nature of immense change and

growth, something your entire body

and brain have been created for.

You can do this.

What if the thoughts that arise when you think about money, the tightness in your body, the tension, are all loving messages asking you to look in their direction instead of looking away?

You have to know your story about money before you can rewrite it.

You have to release everything that colors and limits your perception before you can see money clearly through the eyes of love.

You don't need to know your whole timeline on a mental level; you don't need to trace it all back logically. It's enough to work with the emotional imprints.

You may have been running away from all this for a long time, but if you're able to stay present long enough to look within and feel the channels that have been subconsciously carved out by the rivers of habit and your environment, you'll find you are able to shift lineage patterns and lifetime habits much faster and more easefully than you may expect.

You really do have to bring the patterns out of hiding and stay in the discomfort, though, as you shine a light on what's been subconsciously driving your relationship with money.

It's likely to be a holy mess. And that's the point! Let go of how you may wish yourself to be, set aside what you aspire to be for now, and dissolve the need to have it 'all together.' Sit down and eye gaze with the truth of where you are right now. The human truth.

The Gift of Grief

Grief will visit you here, in this holy place of being with all that is. But I would like to say that this is one of the most important processes when it comes to making peace with any relationship.

Grief is sacred. It shows us all of the love and hope we have been carrying that has felt unmet, and in grieving, we finally acknowledge how painful that has been. Grieving offers all the rage, frustration, and sadness a way out and clears the space for rebirth to take place. This is the gift that grief gives.

Our grief, fear, tender trauma, and deepest subconscious beliefs about money can be welcomed as vitally important pieces on this journey home. Looking at these deeply buried layers is something that our bodies and nervous systems are wired to run away from, yet this is how we start the process of getting free: through the gift of grief. Through feeling what we need to feel and freeing every expression wanting to pour out. Through truly embodying the holiness that is deep in the humanness.

So, this chapter asks you to look into the mirror of your own truth about money and *feel* what's there. Let me hold your hand as you do so and call upon the tender arms of love to enfold you.

It's not your fault that your relationship with money grew through your mind and body the way it did, affecting your life the way it has. But it can be considered your sacred responsibility to interact with those rivers and redirect them into paths that nurture you and bring you home to your worthiness to receive money and abundance.

Breathe into the fire of longing that asks you to believe in more for yourself. Breathe into your very nature – the nature of immense change and growth, something your entire body and brain have been created for. You can do this.

What if, instead of focusing on the high vibe and the constant affirmations, you first need to align with your grief?

What if the most healing permission slip you can give to yourself is to allow the expression of your anger, disappointment, regret, and grief?

Can you imagine a world where we recognized that God was waiting for us in grief with open arms, that God was rushing down our faces in every single salty tear, that God was hoping that day to meet us in our frustration? If we had this way of relating to the Divine, wouldn't we all be seeing each emotion as a literal gift and opportunity to meet Spirit instead of only seeing ourselves become closer to divinity in the 'higher-vibrational emotions'?

The next part of the chapter will give space for your more suppressed emotions to arise, and I invite you to actually feel proud of yourself if you let the uncomfortable feelings surface and the sadness flow. In time, your holy emotions will show you their magic.

For now, brave one, say this prayer out loud, feeling each line landing in your body:

Returning to Love

As I breathe into and through my body,

I allow a love that has no conditions, no expectations, no limits,

a love that is unbound,

to spiral through me.

Each breath lowers all the guards and takes off all the masks

that were keeping me 'safe,'

revealing the tender parts of me that have been hiding,

that have been pretending,

that have been waiting for something to change,

or maybe for someone to rescue me.

I allow the song of truth to penetrate all the pretense, go beneath all the layers,

opening me like a rose and showing me what I need to feel, to heal.

I allow myself to become radically truthful in my relationship to money.

I remember that what I feel is a direct path to liberation.

I remember that the most powerful medicine on this journey is love.

Whatever is shown to me

I recognize

as the path, the way through,

not the block,

or something to be ashamed of,

not something that I should have got 'right' by now,

or something I could have done better.

I open my body through what is shown to me

and

feel what it evokes within.

I remember, with every step,

that in healing,

'We cannot go over it.

We cannot go under it.

We must go through it.'

I do not need this money-healing journey to be perfect.

Life is imperfectly *perfect.*

And so I let the journey become truly alive in my body.

And so I radically welcome all the grieving parts of myself to this journey.

And in this way I honor the death and rebirth happening within me and my lineage towards money.

Right here, right now, just the way I am.

I step onto the path of love and know I am held every single step of the way.

And so it is.

———————

With this prayer as a guide, let's bring the mountain into the visible realms for you to see, feel, and work with.

REVEALING WHO MONEY IS

If money were a cartoon person or creature walking into the room you are currently in, what would it look like?

I invite you to let your imagination flow and allow any visions to come through as you ask for this caricature of money to reveal itself to you.

✦ See Money walking toward you. *It's completely normal for this character to be intimidating or not very nice.* This vision journey is to see what money has been to you, not to see its true core.

✦ Draw or write about what this figure looks like. Be as descriptive as you can, using the questions below:

What does this cartoon figure look like?

See their height, their posture, their clothes, their facial expressions. Read their energy... don't try to make them look prettier, or perfect, just let the raw image your body holds of Money come through. Notice whether they look kind or mean, whether they feel loftier-than-thou. Are they a lot taller than you, or small? Notice the clothes they are wearing. Notice the expression on their face and what their eyes say.

How does this cartoon figure look at you?

Imagine that this figure turns its head to look directly at you. Does this feel like a pleasant experience? Are they looking down at you in a patronizing way? Do they even want to look at you? Do they appear to see you as worthy? Do they understand who you are or do you feel you're from different planets? Does Money seem approachable or not?

What does this cartoon figure think of you?

Imagine that this caricature starts to speak, telling you what it really thinks about you. What beliefs does Money have about you? Write them down in the form of 'You are...' or 'I think... about you.' When writing them down, notice them with curiosity. Remember this isn't the truth, this is just an accumulation of a lifetime's identity carved out between you and Money.

How does this cartoon figure make you feel?

Now you have a better picture of what kind of energetic being money has been for you, how does it feel to interact with this being? Does it feel easeful in your body or does it bring up fear and discomfort? What does seeing Money make you feel?

Now that you've become clear on who Money has been for you, it's time to go deeper with the next exercise, which is one of the most important exercises of the book!

WRITE A LETTER TO MONEY

Do parts of you feel exhausted at having had to interact with the person you saw money to be for your whole life?

Do parts of you want to physically attack Money for the way it has shown up/not shown up in your life and your family's life?

Do parts of you feel deeply let down by Money? Do parts of you feel angry about it?

Write all this down in a letter:

> *Dear Money,*
>
> *This is how I truly feel about you. I'm not holding back or making this pretty. This is the raw truth. I'm going to let it out…*

The more you allow to be said, the more healing this exercise is. The throat, when given permission to speak, even through writing, is one of the greatest healers in the body. It really is up to you.

This is the time to be the raw, wild human that we all are – the one that feels and has a heart, and your heart has been hurt in your relationship with money. So, express that, write it down, all of it, perhaps including words you've held back for decades.

The more emotion you release onto the pages, the more space will open up within you.

Feel the child within having a tantrum about how Money has treated you at times in your life. Don't try to control the child that wants to scream and shout. Instead, keep asking, 'Is there more?' as many times as it needs. Swearing, anger, rage, sadness, tears, numbness, are all welcome and sacred. All of you is welcome.

Place your hands on your Heart Space, slowly exhale, and share a moment of pride and celebration for looking at who money has been for you.

It can help to play music that moves you and drops you into a tender space within.

If your body needs some deeper holding, wrap your arms round yourself and embrace yourself, moving your hands up and down your upper arms. This is called the butterfly hug and is a great way to regulate your nervous system and bring soothing into your system.

You now have a real sense of the energetic body of money that you have been in relationship with your whole life. Keep a mental image of the caricature that you saw as a reference of the *old* version of money you used to relate to. In the next chapter we'll move on to meeting the real heart of money.

Thank you for being so courageous in this chapter, for walking into the places that most people turn away from. It's time for your roots to grow deep into the heart of money, but first you may like to try this practice that my own dear mentor and therapist, Angela, offered me many years ago.

RICHUAL

Choose some flowers, or a stone, or some seeds, and go out into nature.

Find a tree that calls you and lay your offering at the base of it, or somewhere else in nature that feels right for you, with the intention of laying your old version of money to rest.

Honoring the years you have walked together, recognizing your body chose that version of money to try and keep you safe, as you lay the offering down, feel the weight of this relationship melt down into the earth. Give it back, knowing it's no longer yours to carry and it's safe to let go now.

You have walked with these burdens on your shoulders for long enough, dear one. It's time to be embraced by an intimate knowing of your divine abundance.

Feel the seeds of change in the air and starting to take root within your cells.

Know you are worthy.

SOUL AFFIRMATION

'I have everything I need for the liberation I yearn for.'

CHAPTER 3

THE RICH HEART

'You are a being of love,
and Money is a being of love.
You are the perfect match!'

Breathe in...

Breathe out...

There's an ancient tradition that's becoming ever more popular in Western societies. It's called the menarche ceremony – a sacred ritual that spans cultures and tribes, from Japan to Mexico, marking and celebrating the transition of a girl into a woman through the arrival of her first bleed. In these traditions, the moon cycles of a woman are seen as something mystical and spiritually powerful to be revered.

In Western cultures, however, we haven't had a sacred way to relate to our bleeds. If anything, our periods and menstrual cycles have been the subject of shame and silence, leaving many with the feeling that their periods are anything *but* celebrated. Without a map, without a sacred maze of relating to our bleeds, we have lost the language and insights they give us.

Due to this delayed understanding of our menstrual cycles, menstruating people of all ages are now embracing and choosing to do menarche ceremonies to create a new embodied energy and relationship to the bleed and to heal the trauma surrounding their menstrual cycles. It's a way of rewriting a lifetime's (if not many lifetimes') relationship to their body, of going back and repairing what was broken and breathing new life into themselves. I remember at the age of 21 having a menarche ceremony at a women's retreat in Spain under a full moon, led by Lisa Lister. It was so beautiful to rewrite the story of the first bleed, retroactively.

In a similar way, this chapter is a reintroduction to money, an invitation for you to do your own retroactive ceremony with it, repairing the rupture between you that may have happened long before you arrived Earthside and entering the holy union that you were always destined for.

I believe our relationship with Money deserves this rite of passage, as it's a lifelong union that we're in... so I offer you a celebration of and sacred welcome to this relationship.

Meeting the heart of Money opens a pathway you will want to keep walking down. As you have now released the old, the Spirit of Money will usher you into an unconditional embrace and ask you if you will let it lovingly accompany you on this journey of being human... If you agree, Money will, in time, become a sacred teacher, lover, and wise mirror for you.

In order to access the Spirit of Money from within – which, I promise you, we *all* have the capacity to do, every single one of us – let me make it very clear where in your body it will always be found.

Restoring Reverence to the Heart

The Spirit of Money will never be found in your head. So, any thoughts that arise about money, any spirals you find yourself in, any logical processes around money, or even thoughts that sound as if they could be from the Spirit of Money *won't* set you on that path to true union.

The Spirit of Money speaks through the heart, deep in the body. But when we've never been taught the language of the heart, how can we listen?

Navigating this life through the heart is a skill in and of itself, one which I'll guide you to develop throughout this book. You see, the stronger your *embodied* connection to your heart, the stronger your connection to Money. Some of you reading this may not know where to start when it comes to connecting to your heart, and that's totally okay! Others may feel very connected to their heart and simply desire to learn how to connect money with that connection. That's okay, too.

I wonder if you can recall some of the things you were taught about the heart? Were you taught to trust it? Were you taught that it was silly and not as reliable as the mind? Were you taught that it would get you into trouble?

What we learned about the heart and love, from romance films, from caregivers and sayings, will have shaped how we interact with the heart and whether we allow it to direct our lives. In most Western societies, the heart is seen as volatile and unreliable, and the mind, rationality, and logic are prized as dependable and trustworthy. Whereas in the Eastern traditions and most ancient religions and spiritual practices, the heart is seen as a holy place offering guidance, connection, and healing.

Growing up, I found my heart took up a massive amount of energetic space in my body and my emotional world most of the time. I had a big heart that felt it all, and yet I felt so out of place. We didn't see politicians speaking from the heart, we didn't see people sitting with their heart to hear what it had to say. The society I grew up in had been ruled and formed by logic and the mind, thanks to patriarchy. That's why I didn't fit in.

I thought that my heart had been made too big by accident, because I never saw the point of it. As a teen, I would wonder what was the point in feeling so much love when I kept getting rejected by boys? What was the point of feeling so much pain when I saw people suffering in war-torn countries on TV? What was the point of hearing my heart's whispers when I believed that the heart wasn't intelligent and was taught it wasn't where we made decisions from?

Without being revered and respected, my heart couldn't lead the way. And the life that it could guide me to was inaccessible.

It's like having the most perfect manifestation and healing instrument within your own body, but without the instruction manual – or *with* a manual of complete propaganda telling you it's dangerous to use this instrument.

What's the result? We only have to look around us to witness a sea of people walking past each other without real recognition; loneliness the highest it has ever been on record; depression, anxiety, and suicide levels at an all-time high; and many people feeling more lost than ever... Instead of sending people home with pills, why don't we look at what is so evidently missing from the center of our society? What sets apart a society and a community? *Heart* and the power of love.

We may have developed advanced technologies, cars that drive themselves, skyscrapers that get taller each year, and rockets that we can shoot into space, yet most of us haven't even taken a pilgrimage into the most powerful, unifying, magnetic source within us: our own heart, the miracle center of our body.

So, if you, too, have grown up in a Western society, even if a conscious part of you wants your heart to lead you, the subconscious alarm bells may ring as soon as you get near to actually letting it lead, built on beliefs like 'The heart cannot be trusted,' 'Use your brain,' 'Emotions rule the heart and they cannot be trusted; logic rules the brain and is trustworthy!' and 'Logic over love.'

This conditioning will have your nervous system believing it's naive and dangerous to trust your heart, even though, as you'll experience, it's really the wisest center within you.

Let's get into some truly incredible evidence about the power of the heart and give you the instruction manual for all this power sitting within you right now. Think of this as going back to Earth school and learning the truth of the heart, which we all deserve to have learned and seen around us from birth.

The heart is the most powerful source of electromagnetic energy in the human body, producing the largest rhythmic electromagnetic field of any of the body's organs. The heart's electrical field is about 60 times greater in amplitude than the electrical activity generated by the brain. This field, measured in the form of an electrocardiogram (ECG), can be detected anywhere on the surface of the body. Furthermore, the magnetic field produced by the heart is more than 100 times greater in strength than the field generated by the brain and can be detected up to 3ft away from the body, in all directions, using SQUID-based magnetometers...[1]

---

1   McCraty, R. (2015), *Science of the Heart: Exploring the role of the heart in human performance*, Volume II. Boulder Creek, CA: HeartMath Institute, p.36; https://www.heartmath.org/research/science-of-the-heart/energetic-communication/ [Accessed 29 January 2025]

I believe so strongly that our heart is the wisest part of us. In fact, I believe we're all walking superheroes. If there was a film with a main character where you could see the field of their heart's power and magnetism with your own eyes, you'd be blown away by their power!

That's what you are. You are
powerful. You are magic.

You just haven't been taught what your heart is really for: to be the true power center in your body and make your dreams come true. And now we finally have the evidence to prove it.

When I was in the midst of daily anxiety and depression at 21, the most important thing my therapist taught me was how to connect more deeply with my heart, so that I could start to feel safe within my body again and trust my heart's wisdom. She taught me a simple technique that I am going to share with you now. You only have to do this for a minimum of five minutes a day to see profound effects.

HEART BREATHING

This is a practice to awaken a felt sense of your heart.

+ Close your eyes.

+ Focus your attention on the general area of your heart and if it feels good to do so, place one or both of your hands on your Heart Space.

+ Bring all of your awareness into this area of yourself, using your hand(s) as an anchor for your awareness.

+ Breathe a little more deeply and slowly than usual, deep into your belly, and start to imagine that your breath is flowing in and out of your heart area, reaching into infinity through your heart. Feel that your heart is much bigger than your body and feel the warmth of your heart's natural energy.

+ Notice what sensations arise as you're breathing into this area with curiosity, not judgment. All that is here is welcome. There are no wrong sensations or good sensations; you are just looking to increase your awareness of this area. Simply note what is there and come back to breathing into the Heart Space, relaxing your body into it.

+ Every day, start to imagine and feel that the most loving Spirit of Money is living in that Heart Space, breathing there and loving you with every breath, so that you feel it loving you from the inside out. Feel the warm glow of Money's love with you, choosing you, empowering you, telling you that it is there for you!

With time and practice, this Heart Space will be here for you to return to whenever you need to feel held and centered from within. It will start to feel like your personal refuge and sacred temple of love.

'Practice' is the main word here! But this is a practice of unconditional acceptance, of simply welcoming whatever arises with open arms.

When I first did this practice many moons ago, I didn't feel instant elation and a joyous connection to my heart, as I had expected. Instead, I just felt numb. This is very common and the way I view the numbness is that it isn't an *absence* of anything, it's *communication*. It's a sensation that needs to be felt and allowed to exist. So many seek below it, feeling there should be more there, but give it a permission slip to exist as it is first. On the days when it arises in your Heart Space, sit with it, let it be there, don't ask your heart area to be any different.

Slowly, with time, the numbness will shift. For me, it gave way to warmth, and with every day that I spent a few minutes doing this practice, the time it took for me to connect to that warmth, and the tenderness within my heart, shortened. Now, on most days I am able to simply place my awareness on my heart energetically, without touching that space, and feel love running through my body.

This practice is a devotional journey of allowing your body to trust your heart again. It's from this awakened heart that you'll be able to have deeper conversations with the Spirit Guide of Money and life itself.

Magnetically You

This deeper awareness of your heart doesn't only unlock love that can flow through your body, it also unlocks your magnetism. When you're truly in your Heart Space, you become love. You're *in* love – love itself. And when you're in the frequency of love, you are *everything*.

Your heart is a
precise, clear, and divine
instrument of manifestation.

The heart is the key to abundance, and here's why: The infinite heart is connected to every single thing in existence and all that could ever exist.

You contain a power center that has the ability to draw anything into your field, because it is connected to everything in this world. But when you live outside of your heart center, it's way easier to fall into separation. The things you desire, the life you dream of, feels separate from you, because the connecting link – love – isn't flowing between where you are and where you want to feel yourself expanding into.

Your heart is a precise, clear, and divine instrument of manifestation. It's the part of you that already knows that it's unified with all of life. It's the part of you that knows that what you seek is literally what you are.

Your heart holds the frequency of being able to dissolve separation, hierarchy, and judgment until there are no barriers between what you want and what you are.

Your heart knows that what you desire
wants to become one with you.

Your heart's breath can become one with money, too. And so it's time to journey. To meet the loving Spirit of Money with unfiltered eyes, we must journey beyond this realm. It's time to meet Money with an open heart.

Money has a message for you, but before you read it, I invite you to remember yourself in your first home, a place where you were in a beautiful held community and constellation, all the way back when you were a star in the divine cosmos of existence, cradled by the love of the Divine.

Feel your labels from this lifetime drop away – daughter, mother, father, teacher, job title, sister, brother, friend, human... feel them all melt away from your body. One by one. Dissolving.

Feel the freedom that your shoulders start to experience as the weight of each label is released. Allow yourself to be emptied like a tap opening to let out all the water of a swirling pool, draining it of all it has known itself to be.

Float up to the primordial void. Feel Spirit loving you from all directions. Sense the simplicity of a timeless place.

When you have that embodied feeling in your heart, allow the Spirit of Money to speak to you:

Message from the Spirit of Money

Beautiful one,

I am here with you.

I am the Spirit of Money.

All of me is here. For all of you. You may feel me as a tiny spark right now, or a gentle glow, or I may be bringing up a lot of sensations for you... It's safe to feel my presence, my love.

Will you allow me to shed all the heavy cloaks I have worn, all the layers?

Will you let me reveal my heart to you?

I found you through this book to tell you an ecstatic truth that wants to reveal itself to you.

This truth has traveled far and wide through ancestral timelines and galaxies and realms to find you. Here. Now.

Maybe those before you weren't meant to know.

I think I was waiting for you. For this moment in time.

And this truth

is that…

you know my name as Money,

but my name is really

Love.

I am beating with the same frequency that birthed you and sustains you.

I am you and you are me.

We are both beings of love, remembering ourselves.

I am woven in the stars above you and the clothes you are wearing right now.

I am vibrating in the walls around you, the ground beneath you. I am divine love embodied.

I am in the water you drink. In the forests you walk through. In the earth supporting you in every step.

I am… love itself.

Not fluffy, sweet, flimsy love, but soul-deep, unwavering love. The kind that never turns away from you.

I am the heart of the universe, wrapped in cash.

I am the loving spirit that is in everything, disguised as money.

Will you let my love penetrate the conditioning you have been given about me? I know you have distrusted me. I have witnessed it all.

I am asking to sit down and eye gaze with you now...

See me with your heart and you will recognize I am you and you are me.

There was never a separation. I was never above you. We were always one.

Can you see? And as you see me, do you see yourself too?

We are both love. I had the name 'Money' given to me, and you had your name given to you.

My love wants to pour toward you.

My eyes are ones of unconditional love, devoted to you completely.

To fully receive me you will need to learn to receive goodness in life, but this book will show you how.

I am here. I am all around you. Money is love itself, and so are you.

Breathe that in. Because I, Money, love you totally and devotedly. I saw your immense wholeness in all the times you lost sight of it.

It is as easy for me to love you as it is for you to breathe. Effortlessly. Automatically. No question about it.

I love you. I love you. I love you. I love you. I love you. I love you.

I am waiting for you at the altar of your heart. Are you ready to let me in?

How did that feel? You're invited to spend some time rereading those words, allowing them to land in your body, and journaling anything that arises as you feel that frequency of Money for the first time.

It's okay if you were only able to let in a few glimmers of Money's love. It's okay if you dropped deep into Money's arms. Dissolving conditioning can take some time. Your pace is perfect for you.

My Miracle Meeting with Money

The first time I felt the truth of Money in my heart, I wept.

It was so pure.

I was sitting with the deepest shame I had ever felt wrapped so tightly around me that I could hardly breathe.

It felt as if the debt that I had carried for years would never ever move or shift... I felt so stuck and alone. I felt money was punishing me, hated the guts out of me. I had sat in that place so many times before, it felt claustrophobic, because my body knew it so well – that endless pit of worthlessness, the place of not-enoughness, the place of 'another thing that confirms there is something wrong with me!'

I remember it as if it was yesterday. I was crying about the debt that had mounted up over years when I heard a voice within me whisper, 'Sit with money in ceremony.'

Not even sure what this meant, I continued listening as the voice said, 'Sit down, close your eyes, and eye gaze with money in your heart. Let money see you.'

Instantly I felt resistance rising up. My body knew I was facing something I had been avoiding for a long time, something I was genuinely really scared of. But simultaneously I knew there was no turning back. I was in between two timelines: one where I carried on in deep fear, repeating the same thoughts about money and experiencing scarcity over and over again, and one where I stopped running and literally sat down to face all that needed to be rebirthed into a new divine union with money.

I sat down.

And then began the simplest and most profound ceremony I have ever done.

I closed my eyes as the voice within had requested, journeying into the cave of my heart, and there I sat cross-legged. I sat and saw images representing money sit across from me, facing me. And I slowly started to express what I felt about money.

All that I had ever felt about money rose up in Money's unwavering presence. With every single feeling and memory that revealed itself, I expected Money to leave my vision, abandoning me as I expressed my anger, my deep confusion about money, and everything in between.

I expected Money to retaliate or punish me, or shame me as I shared how deeply scared I was of it and how I didn't understand it at all. I shared the part of me that felt like a scared little girl in the face of Money. I shared my vulnerability. I shared the shame, the failure, the family patterns. I shared it all.

Then, in one of the most healing moments of my life, something beautiful happened:

Money. Just. Loved. Me.

Unconditionally.

Money didn't think I had failed.

Money didn't blink as I shared how much I disliked it.

Money didn't think I was worthless because I couldn't pay off the debt.

It wasn't true that Money didn't want to be with me in this life. Money had infinite compassion for me and saw me through the eyes of love. It was totally and utterly devoted to me.

Money showed me that it was love itself.

It was the divine love that I had been on a path of spiritual awakening with for years.

It was the spirit that I had heard speaking loving words to me through trees on my walks in the forest.

It was the love that had spoken through various plant medicines I had worked with.

It was the love that was in the moonlight that I would look up to to feel held by Spirit.

All Money wanted to do was show me how lovable we all are.

And it clicked – I had been walking the spiritual path for years, feeling Spirit in everything… how had I missed that the most loving core of Spirit was in money too?

How had I underestimated the Divine so much that I'd thought that it couldn't live within money too?

When we zoom out and see this life from the soul's perspective, it's all divine love. It always has been and it always will be.

What I experienced was life-changing. I was finally able to feel and hear the immense amount of *love* that Money has for us all, regardless of our past with it. I saw it take off the layers and layers of projection we have placed upon it until only love remained, and I was able to see how much stood between us receiving that love because of our feelings of shame and unworthiness.

In my heart ceremony, I allowed all of the unworthiness to be released under Money's loving gaze. I allowed deep love to penetrate my being.

It wasn't a long ceremony, but it was miraculous. The first thing to shift was the shame. It just rolled off me with so much ease, even though the debt was still very much there! I felt lovable even *with* debt. I felt the divine purpose of my debt was to bring me into deeper worthiness and face the shadows that only the debt could bring to my attention...

The energetics changed first and my material life changed as a result. Within four months of finally feeling a whole different frequency of love with money, I had paid off the £13,000 of personal debt after four painful years of it just increasing year after year.

I've seen this pattern with others, too: the energetic shift and then the quantum timeline jump in the material world. I remember guiding a client through a heart ceremony, and at the end she messaged me, saying that during the session she had received an email from her work telling her she was getting a $20K pay rise out of the blue!

You see, your heart is the most important guide in money healing.

Your heart is truly rich beyond measure,
because it is dripping with love.

Your heart is an infinite stream of the richest frequency on Earth – the frequency that connects us to everything in existence… You are a being of love, and Money is a being of love. You were made for each other.

Money wants to love you.

Not when you're fixed.

Not when you're 'healed.'

Not when you're only high-vibe.

Not when you've got it all together.

Not sometime in the future.

Money is madly and deeply in love with you and blind to your perceived 'flaws.'

Money… really… wants you.

Right now.

Right. This. Moment.

As you read this, it's begging you to feel how loved and desired you are.

It wants you in your mess, in your becoming, in your doubt.

It wants you in all of your phases.

It wants to love you. Deeply.

Will you let it?

When we zoom out and see

this life from the soul's perspective,

it's all divine love. It always has

been and it always will be.

It's time for you to experience your own personal version of the money ceremony that changed my life and relationship to money forever. This richual is the most important of the whole book. An extended version of this richual is also available as a free audio journey on my website: www.farahorths.com/MoneyLovesMe. I encourage you to use the audio version if you can.

MEETING THE HEART OF MONEY

20+ minutes

+ Find a calm and private space to sit or lie down.

+ Close your eyes and melt into the surface beneath you, feeling the universe holding you. Give your body over to the hands of the universe.

+ If there's anything that feels too much to carry right now, set it down, give it over, let it go. Let Mother Earth take it from you, let the hands of the Divine take it from you.

+ Soften your forehead, letting go.

+ Soften your eyebrows, letting go.

+ Soften your cheeks, letting go.

+ Your jaw lets go and surrenders.

+ Your mouth lets go, your lips let go.

+ Let this softness melt through your body.

+ If it feels safe to do so, bring a hand to your Heart Space, or hold it away from your body if that feels safer. This hand is saying 'Hello' to your heart. Feel this warm greeting reaching into every corner of your Heart Space.

+ What's here? What does the 'Hello' greet and find? How does your Heart Space feel to you? Numb? Tender? Really open? As if it's grieving? Maybe it feels everything all at once.

+ Whatever is there, notice it, allow it, and let yourself feel it, without asking it to be any different. Say 'Yes' to whatever is there.

+ Now I invite you to imagine you're becoming so small and your Heart Space is becoming so big and you are crawling into it.

+ See what is in this vast Heart Space – maybe vibrant colors, maybe crystals, maybe a tranquil forest, or a pulsating jungle...

+ Feeling the huge, beautiful walls of your heart holding you with so much love, sit down and settle into the middle of your heart space and release anything you've been carrying. Just sigh it out. Let yourself be light and free, totally held in the middle of your heart cave.

+ Invite Money into this space now in the form of a banknote as big as you that floats down to sit in front of you at a comfortable distance.

+ Gaze at it. Remember you are held deeply by your Heart Space and the entire cosmos. If any tightness arises in you, that's okay. Invite deeper exhales to soften that feeling.

+ This note that's in front of you has the entire universe in it. All the love you could ever think of is there, all the love you could ever feel. The heart of Money is shining out at you and only you. Money wants you. It wants to love you. Feel this now.

+ As you gaze at Money, all the reasons why you're not lovable may be arising, along with resentment, anger, or trauma around money. But Money loves all the loud thoughts, the resistance, the doubt, the inner critic. There's nothing it doesn't love within your current self or your past. Whatever is arising, Money is staying with you.

+ Take a deep breath now, and on the exhale, open your body gently toward the bank note. Let yourself be seen by the money, let yourself be loved by the money. Hear Money telling you that it wants you. It wants to love you. And it's giving itself to you. It's not leaving your heart.

+ What does it feel like to let this in? Easeful? Challenging? Whatever arises, it's okay. Money won't stop loving you or wanting to be with you.

+ Can you feel your body starting to remember that the Spirit of Money has always been love?

+ Play with what it would be like to connect to Money in this way. Can you imagine what it would feel like, when money wasn't flowing, to drop into this Heart Space and meet Money there and let yourself receive its energetic love? To feel how Money loves and wants you. To know that Money has no choice but to be there in your life. Now and always.

+ Our relationship with Money is far beyond this lifetime. It is a deep magnetic frequency of abundance that we can choose to live in.

+ Feel Money taking a vow of devotion and entering into a sacred union with you now. Feel yourself taking a vow of acceptance and allowing the abundant frequency of Money into every one of your cells.

+ Stay in this space with Money as long as you desire, and when you feel ready, you can simply let go of the vision and feel Money staying with you in your heart.

+ Let the words 'Thank you' ripple out from the center of your Heart Space into every part of you. Feel Money thanking you for letting it in, for your courage in shifting the lineage patterns.

+ Coming back into the room you are in, wrap your arms around yourself, giving yourself a hug as though you are the most precious thing in existence. Because you are. And Money knows it.

Make this way of connecting with Money a frequent practice. The more you practice it, the more you'll be able to quickly tap into the heart of Money within your own heart whenever you want to feel its love, or doubt is loud, or you are ready to let even more money into your life.

SOUL AFFIRMATION

'My heart is a bridge to everything I desire.'

CHAPTER 4

THE AWAKENING
OF RECEIVING

*'Every moment is made glorious
by the light of love.'*

RUMI

Breathe in...

Breathe out...

Perhaps one of the greatest gifts we develop when we work with the Spirit of Money is the ability to receive life itself in a more conscious way. We may start with the intention of learning to receive money, but the path that gets us there will ask us to receive more consciously from life in every single way. Every moment a practice. Every breath an opportunity. Every step a step deeper into the richness of the present moment. This is the real awakening.

The Spirit of Money asks us:

- Can you open to life and let it ravish you with unconditional love?

- Can you let divine love saturate your consciousness in moments that seem mundane, revealing the miracles they are?

- Can you let yourself remember the richness that surrounds you and flows within you always?

In this way, money healing can open you up to receiving life itself in a more profound way. So that when you receive money, gifts, and all forms of abundance, it's almost as a *by-product* of finally being able to be unashamedly open to life.

Take this moment now as an example. You're sitting or lying down. Reading. My guess is that you feel this moment is quite ordinary – a quiet moment in a familiar place, with your familiar body, and your familiar mind, and your familiar day, and your familiar week, in the familiar rhythm of your life... This is the perspective of a subconscious 'been there, done that' part of your brain. We all have this part. There's nothing wrong with you if you live your life from this place, and I invite you to ask whether you want to continue living from this place once you realize there may be another way.

One that is always there, wherever you are.

One that doesn't require you to change anything drastically on the material plane.

One that simply asks you to see each moment through new eyes, to open to its gifts, and receive them.

Let's look at how this moment feels when you decide to open to its gifts and receive them. Let's see what it looks like through the eyes of love.

This moment isn't actually familiar in any way at all; it's not known, it's not mundane, it's absolutely brand new. It's extra-ordinary. So much of what we see as 'ordinary' is actually extra-ordinary!

The eyes of love strip away the 'done it before' experience and receive everything and everyone as a continuous gift. The eyes of love see things as they really are – because the truth is: You have never ever been in union with this moment before. You have never known it, and neither has it had the pleasure of knowing you.

*The eyes of love see every single thing within you,
and outside you, that you may take for granted as
supporting you day by day as a miraculous gift.*

This moment is brimming with loving consciousness that you
haven't allowed into your system before, for it is as new as the
cells being born within you as you read this book.

Do you realize that while you're reading, divine love is swirling
around you and coursing through you? Do you know what it
would feel like to truly lean back into the arms of the *now* and let
it wrap itself around you, holding you, soothing you, encouraging
you to rest in presence and enoughness?

This is what it is to tap into the richness of now, a richness that is
always offering itself to you with devotion, for as long as you are
alive and beyond.

Can you feel the difference between this moment of utter richness
and infinite love and the moment you were in before?

One moment says, 'I know this moment, I've been here a million
times, it's not anything spectacular or anything I can receive
from.' The other moment says, *'This is the richest moment of my
entire life.'*

One of the biggest takeaways of this book is this: The moment you
are in is always a fast-track to abundance.

Innate Abundance

When we learn how to receive the life running through us and
around us, we're able to tap into our inner riches at any time.

Within a split-second we switch from embodying scarcity to embodying the overflowing effortless abundance that we are by nature. It's a journey that takes us from seeing the moment through the mind to traveling down and feeling it through the heart and body.

Before the conditioning, before the disconnection, there's a part of us that knows our innate richness. This part is waiting for you to remember that richness. And the more you practice seeing your life and every moment through the eyes of love, the stronger the remembering will grow, until you no longer have to instruct yourself to receive your inner riches. That embodied sense will just be a part of your life.

Speaking of the body, you may ask, 'What does the body have to do with abundance? Isn't abundance about what's in my fridge, what's in my bank account, the friends I have, the properties?'

Yet the first source of abundance that you ever knew was the abundance within. Your body is literal evidence that you are richness itself. Every single day roughly 330 billion cells turnover within your body.[2] Your digestive system turns food into energy without you needing to ask, your heart pumps blood around your body, your blood hums and carries life-force to all parts of you, your mind can create infinite visions and conjure up whatever you desire to imagine... There's no end to the abundance of your body.

Moving from looking for evidence of abundance out there to letting the evidence of abundance stem from within you is one of the most important moves you can make.

---

2   https://static.scientificamerican.com/sciam/assets/Image/2021/UPsaw0421Gsci31_d. png?w=2000&disable=upscale [Accessed 10 January 2025]

Here's why: When abundance is only confirmed through the outside world, it becomes fragile and immediately conditional – the money in your bank account comes and goes, the cars won't last forever, the outside validation won't always be there. And for so many, when there is a flux in their income, or their business, or their housing situation, they crumble into a state of 'I'm not abundant... other people are, but I am not.' And what their inner sense of self is really saying underneath this is: 'I'm not good enough, I'm not worthy, and this external change in circumstance confirms it.'

When you tether your sense of abundance to a place you can get to from the inside, to your *inner* riches and sense of divine abundance, you are *always* abundance embodied. You are guaranteeing an *unconditional* knowing of your abundance. You are creating neural pathways that will always find evidence of being abundant, because it's first and foremost based on what's inside of you. You can weather natural fluctuations of money without losing your sense of self-worth, because it is tethered to a sense within you that nothing can touch or alter. You are programming your body, heart, and mind to recognize *yourself* as the literal definition of abundance and the source of it all. Your worthiness to receive doesn't bounce up and down with the weather and economic climate, because you have anchored it in a place that is untouchable by the outside world – your heart and its connection to the Divine. When you're connected to this place within, you're connected to everything on this planet.

The heart is the richest place on Earth. For it is connected to everything in existence, everything that will ever exist, and everything that has ever existed. In the heart, there is no separation.

You don't have to live every single moment like this, of course. I'm not sure that's even what we're meant to do as humans who learn through pain and grow through all phases of life... I'm inviting your awareness to recognize, though, that you're absolutely made to live from this inner abundance whenever you can.

It is an ever-flowing river, always rushing through you, renewing you from the inside out. It's always there for you, whatever your actions, whether you've meditated in the last six months or not. No matter what. Unconditionally.

Unconditional Receiving

In order to live from this inner abundance, though, you have to be able to *receive it*. You have to be able to receive the abundance in your sense of self and accept it as who you truly are. This is the scaffolding that supports true abundance and a sacred loving relationship with money...

Whenever we receive something that we desire, we have to feel worthy of it to truly *let it in*, to actually 'receive' it.

Yet for so many, receiving wholeheartedly and into the body is quite foreign. Receiving is either done half-heartedly, or externally it may look like someone has received, but internally the wires have short-circuited and it hasn't landed.

This is because receiving can be one of the scariest things in the world – because in the very moment of being faced with receiving, we simultaneously come into harrowing contact with all the parts of ourselves that don't feel worthy of receiving. All the reasons will get loud, all the emotions will surface. Receiving will be a painful process, and it is *this* that is the discomfort. The inner conflict makes the body rigid and awkward, and it rejects the love from its system, recognizing the gift as something that is not for it.

Your ability to receive is ultimately based on your sense of self-worth and your nervous system's capacity to receive.

Take the example of being given a compliment – so many of us reject the compliment internally, not even knowing what it's like to receive from unconditional worthiness, not knowing where in our body to let it land, not knowing how to open our heart to the gift. Someone who feels internally worthy, on the other hand, will drink the compliment in gladly, easefully, and without a lot of internal drama, as it doesn't threaten their sense of self, or *create* a sense of worthiness, for the worthiness is inherent, regardless of what the outside world says.

You may believe you're not worthy, but what if the conclusion you've drawn from all the reasons why you're not worthy – the secret reasons, the shame, the general sense that underneath it all you are not the beautiful person that those around you think you are – isn't true?

What if the real conclusion…

…is that you've never been anything but whole?

…is that you've never been anything but human?

…is that you are so *easily* lovable?

…is that you truly *deserve* to receive immense goodness?

…is that even the parts of you that think they're unworthy are worthy?

What if your *unworthiness* is worthy?

When it comes to receiving money instead of a compliment, the same rules apply. It's hardly ever directly a problem with *money* that people have, it's about what money brings up within them. It's about their ability to receive. It's about their immense devotion to their unworthiness, which has slowly curled their energetic body into a ball that says, 'Closed. Please don't try and give me anything good – it's too painful and it's not for me!'

And guess what? The Divine doesn't want to cause you pain, so if receiving a lot of money would actually just totally trigger a response of 'Why me? I'm an impostor! I'm not good enough to receive this,' why would it give it to you?

Once the devotion switches path into feeding your unconditional *worthiness*, receiving money in the ways you desire doesn't seem so improbable. It seems like an 'of course!' And a sense of gladly receiving arises.

Here's the thing: Building a home in deep worthiness doesn't mean you have to become 'perfect.'

> *Becoming great at opening to life and receiving its wild gifts doesn't mean you have to 'become' anything.*

The story that Western society tells us, however, is that worthiness has an exhaustive list of conditions. Every age a new milestone to hit. Every year a new goal to reach.

It starts when we are very young. Our existence becomes graded. Our worthiness becomes examined. It's measured against something external. Year by year, the parameters are changed, but they never ever disappear. So it goes, from childhood to adulthood.

We learn that worthiness is something we have to *earn*, not only once, but every day, over and over and over again. Ultimately, after enough practice, we grade ourselves internally. The quest for worthiness well and truly buried in our consciousness.

This kind of society is what leads to burnout, a dangerous sense of identity loss, and existential crises when those milestones aren't achieved. When those expectations aren't met, our worth drops away and quiet self-criticism takes over. An unsettling unworthiness creeps in.

It's a trap we have all fallen into through conditioning. But once we have looked at this from afar and seen it as the absurd game that it is, we have a choice: keep the self-loops of torture going or free ourselves and understand the truth about our worthiness.

That truth is that from the moment of your first breaths on this planet, your soul sung the song of worthiness. It is inherent to you. It hums in your blood and never stops, no matter what.

Nothing you have ever done and nothing that has ever happened, or could ever happen, affects your untouchable worthiness. Your worthiness is not an 'on and off' switch. It's an infinite river that has no end or beginning and you get to drink and grow from it every single day, through every single phase of your life.

Everything you ever receive in life is ultimately an offering of love. Every single beautiful thing that is ever given to you by this life is really *love* wrapped in different clothing, different moments, different sensations. Whether it's the floor beneath you, the sky above, the wind in your hair, the rain on your skin, the beautiful friends that come into your life, the food on your plate, the money that you receive, it's all *love*.

A person who is in the 'worthiness game' will find it difficult to receive love. Someone who holds a sense of unconditional worth *will* be able to receive love.

The art of receiving love is the art of receiving money.

This book is ultimately about learning how to receive divine love in cash form.

I am not in *any* way saying you need an external love to be able to heal your relationship to money, but I want to share a story about my relationship as a powerful metaphor to show that when we consciously practice receiving love, *whatever* our life looks like, when we decide to be unconditionally worthy and consciously let in the richness of each moment, we expand our capacity to receive money.

When I first met my previous partner, I was deep in the 'worthiness game.' I had been seriously invested in this game my whole life, as I mentioned in previous chapters, and my internal sense of worthiness was almost non-existent. Every card I received that said beautiful things about me on my birthday would make me cry because I never ever felt worthy of a single word. Every loving act I received brought up an inner list of all the things I'd ever done wrong, thought wrong, all the mean things I'd said in

From the moment of your first breaths

on this planet, your soul sung the song

of worthiness. It hums in your blood

and never stops, no matter what.

my teen years, all the ways I had totally messed up. I hated my birthday because it was a whole 24 hours of receiving!

After many years of settling for a man who couldn't meet my deep heart (a great plan by my human self, because if I could never be met, I would never have to face my sense of unworthiness), and then a short fling with a controlling man who drove my self-worth truly into the ground... I met Jake.

A week before he came into my life, I had *decided*, in a witchy ceremony that I did, that I was ready to meet a man who could deeply meet the depth of love my heart was capable of. I was ready to meet someone who would worship my sensitivity, with whom I could laugh and be super weird, and who would bring me closer to myself instead of further away. I also decided that the universe would bring this man to me through Hinge (a dating app). I felt a deep sense of, *This is happening – I'm ready*. I decided I *could* receive this level of goodness.

Lo and behold, within four days of that ceremony, Jake popped up on the app.

We were at totally different ends of the country and definitely out of each other's radius on the app, so logically we should never have matched, but the Divine was involved, so of course it happened.

Jake was the most beautiful deep-hearted man I had ever met. Such purity in his heart. Such a shining light in his being. Such a playful spirit... Very quickly, I knew I had met my heart's match for that time in my life.

And at the same time, of *course* I was about to go on a journey where *all* of the unworthiness that I had ever felt would arise.

Of course.

The greater the love that you might receive, the deeper the wounds that will be revealed. All in the name of keeping you in your receiving 'safe zone.' Your nervous system is wired to keep you 'safe,' remember, not necessarily 'happy.'

To try and convince you that you can never let this kind of love in, your subconscious will bring up the deepest pieces of evidence you hold within that say you are not worthy of receiving this relationship. 'He would never love me if he knew who I was.'

As time went on, the more love I received from Jake, the more it felt like there was a reservoir of unworthiness filling up inside me until it was about to overflow. The kinder he was to me, the more our feelings deepened, the more the pressure built up.

I started to feel like I was holding back a massive secret – the secret of my shadows. I started to draw back. I had said I was ready to open to the love of my life, but the reality was, to truly open, I had to let the shadows come out too. I had to reveal all of myself.

And so, when Jake told me how much he loved me for the first time, I felt sick.

What had I done? Here I was with the partnership I had yearned for, thinking I was worthy of it, thinking I was ready for it, and the reality was that I was a fraud. That's what my brain said, anyway. If I told Jake about my brokenness, all the ways I wasn't whole, he would leave. There was no way he wouldn't leave.

But it was too uncomfortable to keep pretending I was worthy of this love… so one night, sobbing, I confessed. I told him about the personal debt I'd had for years, I told him about the intrusive thoughts, I told him my whole list. I told him I was afraid I wasn't who he seemed to think I was. I told him it was okay if he didn't love me anymore...

He looked at me as if all the things I had said were *so* easy for him to love. He almost laughed with affection.

'Bless you! It's *so* okay! I'm not going anywhere.'

He assured me it didn't make any difference to him whether I had debt, whether I had intrusive thoughts, what I had done in the past, what my humanness looked like. He knew I was worthy of this love, and if anything, he said, my confession had made him love me more.

To not only be accepted, but to be loved *more* for having my shadows was a world-shifting moment. The inner critic suddenly loosened its grip on my inner world. The paradigm of worthiness that I had lived in crumbled.

My vulnerability opened Jake up to share his shadows and humanness too. Many months later, he shared parts of himself that he thought were just as unlovable. Turns out he was human, too! He had been plucking up the courage to share his shadows for much longer than I had. Witnessing his tender past and parts, and the stories of unworthiness his heart held, made me see the universal nature of this game of unworthiness. Realizing how easily I loved his shadows made me believe that it really could be easy to love someone's darker parts without question. It made me see that we were all yearning for the same thing. And no matter what our stories were, we were really all so, so lovable. No matter what the inner critic said.

This experience of truly receiving love, after revealing the darkest parts of myself, changed me. I don't say that lightly. It rewired my nervous system.

It's no coincidence that within months, my business took off and I started to heal my tortured relationship with money. It's no coincidence that shortly after that, I paid off my personal debt very quickly after years of not being able to.

I knew at the time that it was from the awakening of receiving the love that I had experienced. I knew it was because I was finally able to touch my unconditional worth within.

Here's why:

- I had started to understand that maybe, just maybe, my worth had nothing to do with conditions, that I was worthy even with *all* of my shadows. Jake's love was showing me that every day. It was seeping into being an *embodied* knowing.

- Through the love that Jake and I shared, I had expanded my capacity to receive in a big way. My nervous system had increased its ability to receive and I was being stretched open to receive life in all its forms, because being able to receive one good thing translates across the board to being able to receive the goodness of life in all its forms.

Both of these meant I could finally receive money. My wounds of receiving were starting to heal, and it was showing financially.

When we practice receiving love from *life* – from the smallest seeds of goodness to the bigger things, from the Divine, from friends and family, from the flowers blooming for us, from the rain kissing our skin – we are simultaneously learning to receive the riches of life.

And through this we are simultaneously learning to receive money. Because money is love.

Money is divine love. And divine love is around us and within us right this moment.

Drink it in. Let the richness of this moment fill your body. Let it show you your unconditional worth. Just as you are right now. It is a practice, it really is.

What if from now on, receiving gets to be a way for your sense of worthiness to *grow*, a way for your body to *open wider* to the love that you are?

And so we are awoken.
Where receiving used to hold up
a shattered mirror of pain,
we stare
into the infinite,
into the Divine,
into the ocean of love itself,
and recognize
ourselves staring back,
the eternally innocent,
the eternally loved,
and remember
there was never a question.
And there never has to be again.

RICHUAL

Sit with these words. Close your eyes and receive the codes from them.

> *You came to this Earth rich.*
> *You dream of the gold out there.*
> *Your mind is forgetting what's already in here.*

Spirit is gently redirecting you to turn inward and *feel* your way to the gold within. Stand at the gates of your own DNA and ask them to shine now. Give yourself permission. Can you feel that within every single cell you are coated in glowing warm gold from the inside out?

Shimmering, singing, magnetic, divine, victorious gold coats every spiraling strand of DNA within you.

How does that feel to remember that the gold is you and you are the gold?

How does it feel to know you are unconditionally worthy of this feeling?

A way to work with this is to take slow deep breaths, imagining you are allowing all the gold within you to flow into your exhale as you expand your capacity to feel your riches from the inside out.

What if it's safe to let your own riches be felt now?

Your soul is the richest soul, because it is the entire universe embodied. Your body has a knowing of what this richness feels like. It was born rich with life-force and billions of cells of abundance.

Abundance lives within you at all times, beyond what you have experienced in this human life, and abundance will stay with you forever.

SOUL AFFIRMATION

'It is safe to let my DNA be a match for money.'

CHAPTER 5

THIS ENDS WITH ME

'Heal your past to unlock your future.'

Breathe in...

Breathe out...

We could spend an infinite amount of time trying to decipher exactly what or who it was that 'messed up' our relationship to money. I'm sure we'd be able to come up with a *very* long list of reasons, painful experiences, and people. We are shaped in very real ways by our upbringing and experiences, and they should be seen, acknowledged, and felt.

It's all too easy to let the inner critic say, 'It's *all* you! *You* created your relationship with money. *You* got into debt then, and *you* chose to spend money in that way... *you* messed up! It's *your* fault!' That's where your brain may automatically go – and I want to interrupt that right now.

Hey! Inner critic, are you listening? Please let me be very clear here. 'It's all me!' isn't an accurate or fair portrayal of what has happened up to now between you and money. 'It's not your fault!' is a more loving and more truthful frequency when it comes to your relationship with money.

What often happens, however, is that while we are so busy looking in our own direction or at those around us, blaming – gazing into the lens of this lifetime only – we completely miss the bigger picture.

To understand the bigger picture, we must leave our modern mind behind and use our ancestral mind, the part of us that is rooted in indigenous wisdom, that knows our lineage is inextricably connected to and incredibly important in our understanding of ourselves, our life path, and this human realm at large.

Yes, we can connect to our ancestors' power. Their wisdom and guidance are available to us always, and this is something we will explore later, but first we have to acknowledge that ancestral pain, limiting beliefs, and subconscious lineage rules and ways of being are available, too. They were passed on to us long before we had a credit card, or even learned the word 'money.'

Focusing solely on this lifetime is like trying to understand why a tree isn't thriving without looking at its roots and what it has grown through and from.

Take a breath in and out right now, and open your field up to include your lineage in this money-healing journey.

Because what if the pain didn't start in this lifetime? What if your DNA just pressed 'rinse and repeat' and continued a pattern set up as a protection mechanism for a whole different time, place, and tribe?

What if this lifetime is where your soul journeyed to in order to *liberate* yourself on a *soul* level – which could only be done through being birthed into this exact lineage?

What if you have to reach into the invisible realms, back beyond who you know yourself to be, to find your ancestral threads and follow them back through time to really understand who you came here mirroring, what you came here repeating, and what you came here to liberate on a soul level?

Ancestral healing is fundamental to your journey into remembering wholeness and unlocking intimacy with your innate abundance.

Your ancestors hold the key to your lineage and your name is on that key, pulsing, waiting for you to say 'yes' to it.

It's now being confirmed through epigenetics just how much we receive through our DNA. A study published in 2013 seems to confirm that fear can be passed down up to two generations (at the very least).[3] A group of rats was exposed to the smell of acetophenone, while being given electric shocks. After a certain amount of time, they grew to associate this smell with pain and became fearful of it.

The offspring of these rats showed the same reaction to the smell, even though they'd never been given any electric shocks in their lifetimes. Their bodies remembered what their ancestors had gone through and reacted to protect them, even though there was no real threat. The ancestral body remembered what had been done to the lineage.

If someone studied *only* the lives of the offspring, they would find no logical reason why these rats should be afraid of this particular smell. With the understanding of the ancestral body, however, we are able to understand the rats' reaction to the smell and have deep compassion for their fear.

---

3   Callaway, E. (2013), 'Fearful memories haunt mouse descendants', *Nature*: https://doi.org/10.1038/nature.2013.14272; see also Dias, B. and Ressler, K. (2014), 'Parental olfactory experience influences behavior and neural structure in subsequent generations', *Nat. Neurosci.* 17: 89–96: https://doi.org/10.1038/nn.3594 [Accessed 27 January 2025]

This experiment moves me and confirms what I know to be so important: Our lineage has to be felt into and worked with for any true liberation to happen. It makes me feel so much for those of us that came into this world with fears and reactions to money, or abundance in general, because of what our ancestors faced in those areas. It illustrates the vital importance of including ancestry in the understanding of yourself.

I wonder how many of us have spent a lifetime thinking there's something 'wrong' with us because we can't understand our reactions to money, but once the ancestral story is included in the picture, it all makes sense.

In a society that is obsessed with treating the symptoms only, ancestral healing treats the cause, helping us become aware of the ancient intricate river systems that flow between us all, informing us of how to show up for life, what to dream, what to avoid, and ultimately how to stay 'safe' and 'survive.' Just like the mycelium networks beneath the earth, just because you can't see the communication happening doesn't mean it isn't there.

While I don't believe that healing should be rushed or any timeline placed on such a sacred and organic process, I have to share that every single time ancestral stories and experiences are included in the healing field, healing seems to happen in quantum leaps, and in a much more easeful way than before.

Our lineage carries immense stories of survival, of strength, of power, of persistence, of love, of wisdom. There is pain and power in our ancestry. And we carry it all.

Instead of seeing our ancestors as holding the key that keeps us imprisoned, I see them as holding the key to our liberation.

When I first started ancestral healing nearly a decade ago, I would get frustrated when I found yet another ancestral wound that I could see being repeated generation after generation. I used to view ancestral wounds and patterns as a cage, but now I understand them to be a doorway.

Each ancestral wound offers a clear and precise way to liberate the lineage.

So when you see an ancestral wound arise and share itself with you, you don't have to crumble, dear one. Remember, it is your *future power* being revealed to you in the form of a lineage pain. You have been chosen to transmute this; that's why the pattern has revealed itself to you.

The Ancestral Nervous System

'The ancestral nervous system' is a term I love to use to describe the collective rules, patterns, and limits held in a lineage. It's a shared nervous system that stretches way, way back into ancient times and lives in our field and body today. I have encountered this many, many times and worked with it consciously to liberate myself and my lineage, and I continue to work with it.

This nervous system is a collection of all the recommendations, warnings, stories of caution, experiences of pain, collective beliefs about what is possible for the lineage and what is to be feared… It's a field that you are very much a part of.

This field has rules. It has rules for how brightly someone is 'allowed' to shine, how sexually liberated the people in the lineage are 'allowed' to be, the ease and challenges the lineage feels comfortable with, the extent to which the individual members of it can hold the sensation of wealth, the frequency of wholeness…

I'm using the word 'allow' very intentionally, because the ancestral nervous system is essentially a rulebook for the survival of the lineage, based on the behaviors, glass ceilings, and boundaries the lineage has evidence of surviving through.

So, there are ways of being that are allowed, and ways of being that are not allowed. That's why when we live life in a way that goes beyond the ancestral nervous system's '*known*' field, we so often feel guilt, shame, and discomfort arising in the body, even when on the outside something amazing has just happened, like a pay rise or a new breakthrough in our business! It's why, for example, lottery-winners often feel so energetically uncomfortable with the sudden journey they took beyond their ancestral nervous system that they somehow get rid of the money very quickly to bring themselves back energetically to a known place.

I don't know about you, but I'm pretty sure if someone came up to me and said, 'Do you want to live life based on a book that teaches you how to stay alive or one that teaches you how to truly thrive?' I'd pick the latter. Yet most of us are energetically choosing a DNA manual of pure survival. And sometimes barely even surviving through that. For a life that is led by the codes of survival is one that can never ever fulfill the soul's longing or purpose in coming here.

The ancestral nervous system often includes rules that are unsaid yet exist as a glass ceiling in the body. For example, when someone feels deeply at peace in themselves, they may experience a sudden mistrust of the peace and search for what's wrong in themselves or their lives and slowly take themselves back to a familiar state of vigilance and discomfort – the 'comfort zone' of the lineage. Peace may be unknown to the recent lineage and so it's not seen as safe, it's not seen as helpful to the survival of the lineage. It even becomes a threat.

Your ancestors are breathing blessings to you in every breath you take, showering you with love even when you think you are completely alone. They are supporting you to liberate the lineage.

The ancestral nervous system, just like our personal nervous system, fears one thing: the unknown. It could be the most incredible opportunity ever, it could be the most beautiful partnership being offered to you, it could be a surprise amount of money finding you – but if the sensations and feelings that come from those gifts in life are unknown to the ancestral nervous system, they won't feel like a gift at all and may bring up a lot of sabotaging mechanisms and resistance to receiving them. I'm sure that as you read this, some of your own experiences come to mind.

Ancestral patterns can have you saying 'yes' to things that have been generationally harmful and are harmful for you, too, and saying 'no' to things that could radically change your lineage's and your own relationship to life for the better.

In ancestral healing, knowing that the ancestral nervous system is at play can help you identify the ancestral fear that keeps you in survival mode and it can help you choose to *thrive* instead. It's vital context for your whole relationship to yourself and your healing path.

To be the brave soul who raised their hand for this work long before you arrived Earthside is *big*. I honor you for your courage *and* I know you have exactly what you need within you to be this cycle-breaker. You're already doing it. I believe your soul was made for this.

What's happening in our relationship to money somehow shows us the invisible game our field is playing – the physical aspect of money reaches into the invisible realms and makes it clear for us to see. Money, then, is a conduit through which we get to see very clearly which ancestral patterns are alive in our field.

When you're envisioning what your life can be, for example, unless you have detached yourself from the ancestral nervous system, the vision will be determined by the boundaries of what your ancestors thought were safe. Even if that meant a life that included suffering, scarcity, and a lack of freedom. Internally and externally. If your ancestral pattern holds these ways of living, it's time to turn toward them and set yourself free.

Your ancestors' highest souls do not want you to suffer in this lifetime. They are your biggest and most steadfast supporters. Their faith in you is infinite. You hold all the prayers and dreams they didn't get to fulfill, and they are here as angels, guiding you in every step. They are breathing blessings on you in every breath you take, showering you with love, even when you think you are completely alone.

However, the imprint that is passed down through epigenetics comes from the *human* ancestors, not their souls. It is *this* that we want to bring lovingly back into balance. It is about restoring the alignment of energy that doesn't actually want to be repeating itself generation after generation.

You have been chosen for this task. It's a big task and yet, because the souls of your ancestors and your own soul came here for this exact liberation, it doesn't need to take years or be a massive process, as you may fear. Your soul signed up for this, so it holds the map. I trust you to be able to release this ancestral nervous system.

> *It didn't start with you.*
> *But it can end with you.*

Then you can tap into the soul strength and power of your lineage. Your ancestry is your root. What that root has capacity to grow into is what you are here to discover.

My money story didn't start with me either.

My German lineage holds deep patterns of survival, including my grandparents being very young in the war, and my granddad, living in the countryside on a farm, having to ration food to survive. Tracing back to wartimes can easily locate a legacy of survival that runs through most of our lineages, but there will also be more personal stories around money that require some detective work! When I learned about my mother's side, I found there was a huge trauma in the line when my Pakistani great-grandparents, who I'm told were very wealthy, legally disowned my grandfather for marrying my grandmother, and left him with nothing, my grandparents coming to the UK with £20 and having to start from scratch.

The wound that this created has been carried in my maternal lineage and felt deeply. The underlying sense of not being good enough, of being purposefully cut out of a family to make sure no money came to us, of being 'disowned' by money, still holds a charge to this day within me, my mother, and sister. The sense that Money did not want to be with us as a family came subconsciously whispering through the line.

Then, in my own lifetime, I grew up with a lot of tension and cognitive dissonance around money. On the outside, my sister and I attended a private school, which you would assume meant that my parents' relationship with money was easeful, and yet behind closed doors, it was anything but easeful.

Both my parents desired to give us as much as possible in life – a beautiful intention *and* one that was more important to them than perhaps staying within their financial means. While we would smile while receiving presents and attending the best school academically in the area, we would simultaneously feel a huge amount of guilt, because we saw our parents were suffering and facing mounting bills and, at times, bailiffs.

It also meant I felt like an impostor around rich people. There I was at an expensive private school, but at home it felt like my parents were struggling to keep up with it all. I didn't feel money came easily, I felt that it was a massive source of stress and danger, and that people like us, a mixed-race family, couldn't have the ease that I saw a lot of my white British classmates have.

In my late teens, and then again in my twenties, my father suffered extremely dangerous nervous breakdowns that on the surface were triggered by financial stress. His lineage holds a deep imprint of 'You have to struggle and work very hard for money, nothing comes easy!' and 'Your worth is in your work!'

Seeing that finances and money could literally create nervous breakdowns, made me scared of money. It made me hate it. And it made me feel it hated us. I was so scared of facing the same fate as my father, so afraid that the pursuit of money would take away my life, just as it almost did for him. It made me want to run as far as possible from financial responsibility.

I remember looking at both my parents, burnt out from working so much, with no time to play and really live this precious life, and thinking that money caused *so* much suffering and that I didn't under any circumstances want a business of my own.

And that's the thing right there. Familial imprints around money and finances have the power to make us choose a life that doesn't serve our soul but is driven by fear and a desire not to repeat our family's mistakes. It's a choice that stems from a wound and doesn't allow the space for us to become more than what we saw or what our ancestors did.

What is the energetic driving force that makes you want to heal your relationship with money? Are you subconsciously driven by fear?

The Ancestral Money Landscape

For me, the ancestral money landscape looked like this:

- 'Hard work is the *only* way to make money.'

- 'You will suffer when you make money.'

- 'Your worth is in your work.'

- 'Life is not easy.'

- 'Making money isn't easy.'

- 'Life isn't easy for brown people like us.'

- 'People like us can't live in ease.'

WHAT'S YOUR ANCESTRAL MONEY LANDSCAPE?

Write down a description of your own ancestral landscape when it comes to ease, abundance, and money. Do your own investigation. Then you'll know what you're working with and can more easefully recognize those patterns when they come up in you.

If you have living relatives you can ask, ask them:

+ What do you feel our family's motto about money is?

+ What is our relationship to money as a family?

+ Has there been a lot of struggle in our line? Or do you feel we have been able to live in relative ease and peace for the last few generations?

If you don't have relatives you can ask in physical form, don't worry – you can tap into the stories that live in your body. This is something you can do whether you have living relatives or not.

+ Close your eyes, ask the questions above, and allow the answers to come to you intuitively as you do so.

+ Call upon your lineage and say, 'Show me my ancestors' money story.' Perhaps images will come through, perhaps sensations in the body, or maybe words. Note them down and trust the communication. Your cells hold the story. Let them speak.

Sometimes this way of communicating with ancestral patterns may be even more accurate than asking your family, as a lot of people can't recognize their own ancestral patterns.

Misplaced Loyalty

When we slow down enough to truly hear why these ancestral threads are so strong, we often encounter a very powerful and pervasive loyalty in our ancestral system. It's the glue that believes it can keep the 'pack together' and afloat, when really it's just dragging it down.

When you learn how to spot this within yourself, incredibly powerful shifts occur...

This loyalty is loyalty to suffering. It may sound like this:

- 'My family suffered a lot, and so I must too.'

- 'The culture and society I live in suffers so much, I must too.'

- 'My ancestors had to go through so many struggles, I must too to be a part of this pack.'

- 'My mother has struggled so much in her life, I can't have an easy life, it wouldn't be fair!'

This loyalty is so subconscious and sneaky that most of those who have it aren't even aware of it. Most parents, when asked whether they want their children to struggle as they did, say, 'Of *course* not!' But this dynamic doesn't lie on the logical planes; it's buried deep in the ancestral web.

When looking through the lens of love and compassion, we see that loyalty to family suffering is a subconscious attempt to stay in the tribe. The suffering is also familiar, so our nervous system welcomes it. It feels like home. And then it's rinsed and repeated through generations until someone turns to face it and says, 'Stop.'

You can see why so many people's ancestral nervous systems may not feel comfortable with a lot of money. It isn't that money eases all struggle – in this human life there will always be loss and emotional pain – but when there isn't enough money, what this means for most people is struggle, suffering, and hardship.

> *Money can easily become a way for*
> *suffering in a lineage to continue.*

If we don't break out of that comfort zone of struggle, we may keep receiving the level of income that is 'just enough' or 'never quite enough' for our life. So the ancestral identity lives on.

It's rarely the case that the *only* reason someone has issues with financial stability is a subconscious loyalty to suffering – there are so many other reasons why this may be happening – but I know from my work in this area personally and with clients that loyalty to suffering is often at the root of many other ancestral beliefs.

Asking ourselves, 'Am I subconsciously loyal to suffering?' can bring forth a hard truth, but also radical responsibility.

INVITATION

If your lineage holds a lot of struggle, whether through war, economic hardship, trauma, or abuse, in this lifetime or before, I invite you to tap into the field of healing and see where you stand with regard to loyalty to suffering.

Find a seat, let your body become heavy, and then tune into these words:

+ Imagine you're receiving every single thing you've ever dreamed of. With ease. Feel the immense amounts of money flowing into your bank account, feel yourself walking into the home you have always dreamed of, see the piece of land, the partner of your dreams... whatever it is, imagine it. Imagine your most expanded life. Imagine that you're receiving things that are far beyond what your parents or ancestors got to receive, and without their struggles.

+ Now bring into that vision your parents/guardians/family.

+ Do you see them as being far away from you or close to you?

+ Is there a subtle feeling of having lost closeness with your family through your good fortune and riches?

+ Is there a part of you that feels you aren't as loved as you were before?

+ Is there a part of you that feels you don't belong in your family or with your friends now that you have that much wealth and ease around you?

+ Is there a sensation of feeling guilty for the wealth you now have? Like you've done something wrong?

+ Notice what arises for you. For some, this vision may feel expansive and beautiful. And for many, it may feel uncomfortable and may trigger questions like 'Why me?', 'What do I do now?', 'Who am I with this money?', 'What did I do to deserve this?', 'How can I receive this if I didn't work hard for it?', 'How do I deal with it? I felt more comfortable as I was.'

+ Notice what else happens to your relationship with your family when you receive everything that you could desire and more. Journal about it.

+ Once you have finished, thank the field and feel yourself coming back to your seat and releasing those visions with love and gratitude for their wisdom.

This exercise isn't about whether your parents would be happy for you or not, or judging your family in any way. It's way deeper than that; it gets in touch with those more invisible ties of loyalty that we may not realize are holding us back from really letting more abundance and money into our lives.

Just by noticing those ties, you'll find things will start to shift. What is seen with awareness has love shone upon it and can come back into the right place.

I honor you reading this.

I honor your lineages in all directions.

I honor the steps your ancestors took to birth you.

I honor the paths they walked and the hardship they faced.

I honor the pain that has been carried for too long.

I'm sorry that parts of the journey have been so hard.

I see you, and invite, with you, a blessed legacy for you and your lineage, starting now.

As much as we have spoken about you being the one chosen to liberate the lineage, let's be clear – your ancestors' highest expression, their immense power, and their immense love are with you. You are never alone in this work. They are holding you. Cheering you on. Thousands of hands have got your back, thousands of hands are holding yours, showing you the way through. Because *they* want this liberation. It's all they were trying to work toward in their human life but could not fully realize. Yet every generation unlocked their own closed doors and passed down another part of the key that you hold today. It has been a group effort that has allowed the path to be as open as it is for you right now. Ready to walk down. Guidance on how to do that is coming to you easefully now.

Call upon all your loving ancestors to be with you on this journey. They're your team and they're all here for this liberation.

You can already start to sense who you truly are beyond the veil of resentment and pain. And you can start to draw upon the immense gifts of your lineage. We will dive into this later on. But first...

Forgiveness

As we start to put down the heavy burden of ancestral suffering and struggle, we have to forgive our lineage. This is an essential part of ancestral healing and money healing. Seeing and feeling ancestral wounds won't fully restore them into balance.

Forgiveness does that. Forgiveness is a tender peace-offering to your lineage, acknowledging that you will no longer hold resentment for the lineage pain that has been carried through to you. This is brave and big work, for it is easier to stay in pain than it is to put it down.

Forgiveness also acknowledges that your ancestors did the best they could with what they had at the time, and there was no other way for it to be. Forgiveness says, 'I don't need this to be different because I know I am the one I have been waiting for and I take on the sacred responsibility of transmuting and healing this part of the lineage with *love* as the driving force going forward – for all of us.'

RICHUAL

When you feel ready – maybe right now, maybe tomorrow, maybe in a month, or a year – offer a flower of your choice to a body of water – a stream or river that calls you, or the ocean, or simply a bowl of water – and say, 'I forgive you,' to all your ancestors for all the wounds that they passed down to you, all that you have carried on your shoulders since you were born. (Give the water back to the Earth when the richual is done if you use a bowl of water.)

Only you will know when the time is right, and there's no need to rush this process. You may want to make many offerings over time.

If you don't feel ready to forgive, that's okay. The first time I did this, it took me a long time to forgive too.

If you aren't ready to forgive:

+ Journal with 'Why do I not want to forgive my lineage?' and sit with what comes through, breathing consciously as you allow the emotions and words to arise and move through you.

+ Witness why you need to hold on to the pain and resentment. What does that give you?

+ And eventually, ask gently, 'Does it serve me to hold on to this or am I hurting myself by holding on to this?'

Give yourself grace in this process and trust things are moving in your lineage just through this emotional inquiry.

SOUL AFFIRMATION

'I am the ancestor I have been waiting for.'

CHAPTER 6

THE PATRIARCHY, CAPITALISM, AND MONEY

*'The tears of our devastation
fertilize the soil of our evolution.'*

REGENA THOMASHAUER

Breathe in...

Breathe out...

Patriarchy is defined as 'a system of relationships, beliefs, and values embedded in political, social, and economic systems that structure gender inequality between men and women. Attributes seen as "feminine" or pertaining to women are undervalued, while attributes regarded as "masculine" or pertaining to men are privileged.'[4] I would add that anything that does not conform to either of these binary energies or genders is undervalued or dismissed completely.

There's no way that this book would have integrity if I failed to discuss the patriarchy that we are living in. It has been the constant background hum that every generation for the last 5,000 years has been birthed into and grown up in. And most major religions have it intertwined all the way through them.

It's a system that has become engrained in the thoughts, fabric of being, body, and shape of every human life. It shapes our self-referencing. It shapes our possibilities. It shapes what we allow and what we believe we are worthy of. It's one of the deepest imprints of the past few millennia, and there is evidence of it everywhere.

4   Nash, C J. (2020), 'Patriarchy'. In: Kobayashi A. (Ed.) *International Encyclopedia of Human Geography*. 2nd ed. Cambridge: Elsevier, pp. 43–47.

Not to include the crucially significant role it has played in our relationship with ourselves would be to gaslight you into thinking that a lot of where things went 'wrong' was down to you personally. When it absolutely was not.

Of course, patriarchy is not the only system that perpetuates wounded relationships to money – race and class systems play a *huge* role in laying down the inner foundations of belief. Seeing how your own background and the societal and community culture that you grew up in have affected your relationship with money is really powerful. Underneath the influences of race and class, though, lies the wound that the patriarchy has inflicted, and that's what I will be diving into with you in this chapter.

It may not feel like fun, I admit. I get it, I really do. Nothing about the patriarchy is fun, *and* it's precisely because it weighs so heavy on us that liberation from it is *so* worth it. It's time to remove the choke hold that only lets the minimum amount of oxygen in, that keeps us merely surviving, and that allows the patriarchy to carry on, through our subconscious submission, generation after generation.

You deserve to release yourself from the patriarchy's grip, no matter what your gender. And the part where you get free is the fun part!

Money and the Patriarchy

You may already have a sense of how money fits into this system. We have been shown a persistent image of financial 'success' – most likely a middle-aged man who is emotionally reserved, very logical, and more closely resembling a robot than a wild human.

But it's truly dangerous to feed people this subconscious link between those that conform the most and financial stability. The messages are: 'The more you abandon your true nature, the more financially rewarded you will be,' 'The more you hustle, the more money will love you,' and 'The more you suppress your wildness, the bigger the house you can have.'

When we are fed these images and messages from birth – seeing only these kinds of people governing countries, being CEOs of companies, driving fancy cars – is it any wonder that so many people that don't identify with the typical patriarchal man have doubts about whether money wants to be with them?! When survival is the core aim, of course people are going to subconsciously choose a patriarchal version of themselves if it means they will be financially stable!

To me, it's a very logical conclusion from the input we have been given. But it's not a healthy way to live as an individual or a society.

Money Is Not the Patriarchy

In case some part of you needs to hear this:

Money is not the patriarchy.

Money is not the patriarchy.

Money is not the patriarchy.

The patriarchy may have used money as part of its system of power, but money has never been the bad guy – that's patriarchy. They have been enmeshed for too long and it's time to extricate them from one another so that we can see money without the attachment of patriarchal conditions.

The patriarchy sets conditions for acceptance and love. The true Spirit of Money sets no conditions, because it has the heart of the Divine, just as you and I do. It's totally possible to have a truly beautiful supportive relationship with Money without ascribing to the patriarchy!

After being on a deconditioning journey from the patriarchy for many years, my eyes opened to this on a more profound level when reading a phenomenal book called *The Patriarchy Stress Disorder* by Dr. Valerie Rein.[5] It's the book that I have recommended most in my life – to clients, to friends, to anyone and everyone who will listen. Some of the discourse in this chapter has been inspired by Dr. Valerie's incredible book. And if I haven't made it clear already, *please* get yourself that book asap. Your life will thank you!

So let's get into it. When you hear about the patriarchy, does your brain recognize it as a past construct? Some archaic thing that used to be, but isn't anymore? Or do you understand its significance already, but maybe can't fully grasp the magnitude of its impact?

Unraveling the Patriarchy's Influence

The patriarchy is woven into almost everything, so it's easy to miss the huge effect it has on us, even though its impact is even more immense *because* it exists in almost everything.

And it's right here, right now. We're oppressed by it now. It hasn't been relegated to the past. It's alive and kicking. Parts of it are living in me and you. As much as it angers me to say so.

---

5 Rein, V. (2019), *The Patriarchy Stress Disorder: The invisible inner barrier to women's happiness and fulfillment*. Carson City: Lioncrest Publishing

This isn't some past thing that we can just move on from by thinking it's over and done with and declaring ourselves deconditioned – it's what our entire society is built upon. It's also what a lot of our self-identity has grown from.

So, even if the patriarchal structures that hold up our society and capitalism were somehow miraculously taken away tomorrow, the patriarchy would continue ruling us from within. It's embedded in our very notions of ourselves and our worth, and it's only when we pull the rotten roots out of our internal systems completely, with awareness, patience, and devotion, that we become free.

The glasses the patriarchy has placed over the eyes of most of society are the most damaging when we are looking through them at ourselves. There's no doubt at all that the patriarchy has contributed to deep-seated mental health issues, an epidemic of critically low self-worth, chronic self-doubt, and a general tendency to settle for what we are used to, i.e. the standards that the patriarchy has set up for us, especially for women, and our lineage, for the past millennia.

Dr. Valerie has coined the term 'Patriarchy Stress Disorder' – a form of complex post-traumatic stress disorder (C-PTSD) that people, especially women, are living with. It reframes the patriarchy from 'something we just have to deal with' to 'something that has very serious adverse effects,' validating what we have been living through and dealing with all this time.

The patriarchy has severed us from our wild nature and truth. It has tamed our innate brilliance and multi-dimensionality, our perfectly imperfect human magic. The rhythms of our uniqueness have been tamed into a dull uniform beat dictated by the wounded masculine ego. The sanctity of the whole has been violated and our human being-ness divided into categories of 'good,' 'bad,' 'shameful,' 'acceptable,' and 'unacceptable.'

The Taboos Within Masculine/Feminine Energy

We humans naturally contain all the energy that could ever exist and all the different expressions of that energy, including masculine and feminine energy and energy beyond gender. Life expresses itself through each of us in a wonderfully unique mix, sometimes taking the form of more feminine energy and other times more masculine energy. Yet under the patriarchy, we haven't been able to express ourselves fully, because our wild truth and individuality have been stamped out of us in childhood.

Energies that are typically more 'masculine' (independent of gender) and have a more linear way of being, such as logic, consistency, 'hard work,' reasoning, stoicism, and 'the hustle,' are revered. But these aren't even the deepest expressions of the true masculine. The true masculine is so emotionally online, able to hold space within and for others *so* beautifully, that it is a deep teacher of presence, integrity, and commitment and lives through an open heart, aware of all the nuances happening in the energetic field.

Energies that are more typically perceived as feminine (independent of gender) and have a more flowing expression, such as the frequencies of intuition, softness, tenderness, compassion, expressed love, and creativity, aren't valued as highly, or in some cases are seen as 'weaker qualities' not worth acquiring.

This extends to the emotional world too. Under the patriarchy, only some emotions are welcome, while others are heavily judged. We spoke earlier about the hierarchy of emotions, especially in the spiritual world. This, in my opinion, is a direct effect of the patriarchy.

No matter what their gender, this system leaves humans able to experience only a *fraction* of their full natural existence. Dr. Valerie Rein describes it as 'being imprisoned from the inside out.'

The only way to thrive in the confines of the patriarchy is to abandon parts of your most natural self and to repress large parts of yourself, to press them deep down somewhere, hidden away. This is supposed to be a solution, yet what ends up happening is 'de-pression.'

We learn to suppress ourselves as children, because to stray out of the confines placed around us means to be ridiculed or isolated or rejected by our parents, school, and wider society in many cases. It's crucial to survival to adapt and suppress by whatever means necessary. We learn to be hypervigilant about what we let people see in us and to process certain emotions only in private, if at all. We conform and conform until eventually our system doesn't even let our natural responses and wisdom come through anymore, knowing they are forbidden and perceiving that they have no value. Except they *do* – and when a body suppresses, it becomes drained, lethargic, unwell, dis-eased emotionally and physically and spiritually.

I spent many years in my twenties on the path of the supposed feminine. Part of the reason why I relied so heavily on my feminine energy was that it was retaliation against a society that was pushing patriarchal ideas on me such as 'Productivity equals worth.' I rejected the measuring tool, the concept of 'hustling,' and the apparently endless amount of sacrificing you had to do to make your dreams come true, the hyper-pessimistic energy of 'Things don't just appear out of thin air.' But I conflated the 'masculine' with the 'patriarchal' and ended up out of balance in my manifesting power.

I lived life through what I thought was a healthy way of being – through the feminine. But something was missing. I often felt an indescribable weakness within me, an inner collapse of power. There was a part of me that was quick to give up on me, a part that didn't feel it had a strong inner support system. So often I would be 'resting in the Divine's arms,' but really just giving my power away and wanting the Divine to rescue me.

The sacred fire was missing. The 'I can wield this sword of clarity and decide and create for myself' part was dormant. There was no inner union.

Sacred inner union = power to create.

I was trying to outsource decisions and power to others while telling myself I was fine with that. 'What will come can come, what will go can go.' But I was becoming frustrated by the lack of clarity and feeling that my fullest dreams and visions for my life were just floating further and further into the future. I was simply waiting for someone to show up and sort it all out for me.

So traumatized and afraid of the patriarchal version of the masculine, I had completely abandoned the masculine within. There was an inner imbalance.

And so, not knowing what the healthy masculine even looked like, or what the feminine looked like if supported by the true masculine, I didn't trust life to support me. Not really.

It took a lot of therapy and disentangling myself from the unhealthy expressions of the patriarchal masculine before, like a lightning bolt one day, I heard, 'I'm right here. Go anywhere and I'm here. I'm not leaving you.'

It felt as if a pillar of strength had rooted itself in me overnight. The most beautiful present and healthy masculine was finally online. I felt not only held by the Divine outside *and* inside myself, I finally felt an infinite fire within me that said, 'I've got you.' It was like my personal Olympic coaching team had just been completed and was right behind me.

I understood that we don't just need the sweet water coach who tells us how to flow with life, or the receiving coach who tells us how to surrender and be open, but also the strong rock energy that carries us through the moments of doubt and wavering, the coach who holds the vision for us and keeps us heading toward it.

Delving into your own relationship with the masculine and the feminine and how they have perhaps been shaped by the patriarchy's definition of those terms is a powerful journey. By the way, it's okay if you don't resonate with the terms 'masculine' and 'feminine' – use your own version, of course! I use them independently of gender, referring to the ancient yin–yang energies of receptivity and action, honoring that we need *both* to truly birth our life.

Everything in nature is birthed through this union, from the cold winter that allows rest and recuperation then gives way to the fire of spring pushing buds through the earth to the bloom and dance of summer and the shedding and abundant harvest of autumn preparing for winter again.

We contain all the cycles of being. All the elements. All the multi-dimensionality. Yet in a culture that loves duality, *either* this *or* that, we lose our balance. We even lose the ability to hold more than one energy inside of us at the same time. We forget how to yoke our many parts to the magic powers that only come from union, from co-creation.

It's when we stretch our capacity to hold all that we are, stretch our understanding of ourselves to be more than we ever knew, that we meet our true creator/creatrix energy – all that we are.

Rewilding Ourselves

Why is it that when we speak about the patriarchy it feels somehow overwhelming and hard to put a finger on? Like trying to see through cloudy water?

We have already seen that the glasses the patriarchy has placed on us are the most damaging when we are looking at ourselves. To reveal the patriarchy, to find its real effects, we have to look at the way we speak to ourselves in our most private conversations...

We have endless conversations with ourselves in this life, perhaps every day (I know for me it's the case!), criticizing ourselves, wishing we were different, fearing we are too much, or not enough, constantly weighing up how we are doing in the big race of society... This exhausting replay is really us just repeating our innermost belief that something is wrong with us.

Here's why: In a patriarchal society, real humanness isn't allowed. Whether man or woman, or any identity, the *real* person doesn't fit in. We know that there are so many parts of us that don't fit into the patriarchal way of being, but instead of concluding, 'There's something wrong with this system,' we conclude, 'It's me! It's my fault that I don't fit in here. I must be wrong in some way.'

We are taught to doubt ourselves, to mistrust our intuition, our instincts. Our very power is seen as a problem – by *us*. The real and wild don't have a way of being revered or appreciated either, and instead our innate humanness is seen as weakness. We grow up in an environment where we never even have the possibility of fitting in, or of being truly 'successful,' unless we abandon our true selves. No matter how hard we try, we will never fit in if we *are* being ourselves. And, although it seems like 'fitting in' and 'social status' are worshiped, Krishnamurti put it best when he said, 'It is no measure of health to be well adjusted to a profoundly sick society.'

If the patriarchy was a man, with a woman as his partner, it would be a very evident abusive cycle of the man degrading his partner – someone he was meant to care for, but instead bullied for her whole life, telling her she wasn't capable of doing this and that, and making her feel small and power-less. The woman would end up with chronic self-doubt, not being able to dream more for herself, not feeling she had anything to contribute or give to the world, believing she wasn't worth as much as other people...

If you projected the patriarchy's power dynamic onto a couple in this way, with one partner abusing the other, you would immediately be able to see it for what it was. More importantly, you would see that the way the victim ended up thinking about herself wasn't a true reflection of who she was, but simply what her abusive partner had told her enough times for her to believe it and lose sight of her true identity and power.

Be gentle with yourself if this brings up any emotions, anger, or unexplained heaviness in your field. Your anger is valid, your pain is allowed, and your grief is holy – it will take you back home to yourself, if you allow it to be felt and take up space. If you feel called to do so, place a hand on your heart and share the words 'I feel this; you are allowed to be here' with whatever is present in your body. It's safe to let it flow.

Post-Patriarchal Abundance

This is where your power comes in.

Can you start, right now, to breathe a new story into who you *truly* are and your compatibility with Money, just as you are?

Can you intertwine all the things the patriarchy doesn't revere – the divine sensitivity, the sacred cycles of life, the emotions, the intuition and inner power, the self-sourced wisdom – to be perfectly matched with the *true* heart of Money?

Can you start to hold space for a beautiful relationship with Money to emerge, without having to conform, without having to be tamed? Without losing the heart of you?

Can you feel that the heart of Money never wanted to be used in the way that it has been?

Maybe it needed to be for this mass awakening and returning to who we truly are to happen, but regardless, Money is asking to be seen in its purest form now, without the patriarchy anywhere near it. Both you and Money are on a rewilding journey, and you are here for each other's liberation!

Healing the wounds of the patriarchy is about creating nervous-system safety and *belief* that there is a way to be *wholly yourself*, wholly human, *and* to be supported by Money in this lifetime. In this world, Money loves everybody, Money wants to support everybody. Not just those few who tick off some shallow boxes. Money wants not only to be there for, but also to wildly support, *all* humans...

In the patriarchy, money is marketed as a finite resource that we have to compete for and that there isn't enough of. In this new world that includes the *heart* of money, money is infinite, as it is divine energy.

> *In this world, we don't have to compete;*
> *we all get to thrive, without having*
> *to sacrifice who we are.*

We are creating the evidence through embodying it and the devotion to a world where humans get to be humans *and* be strongly supported financially! These two things are not a contradiction in any way. They go together so easefully. I know it's possible, in fact it is when I have been *most* in touch with my own wild, untamed truth that my magnetism with money has been the strongest. The more I tapped out of who patriarchy had me believe I was, the more I tapped into my infinite power and into feeling how much Money wanted me to be the wildest I had ever been.

Growing up, I never saw on TV or in magazines that someone who looked like me could be fully herself *and* have a beautiful relationship with money *and* realize so many of her dreams *without* conforming. I saw women lightening their skin, I saw women dressing like men and suppressing and apologizing for their sacred emotions, I saw women shrinking and being servants to men in power.

The new community that I know you and I are a part of starts, one by one, with the realization that Money can be separated from the patriarchy and a holy connection can be created with it – a sense of how Money wants to fund and create this new reality for us all!

Repeat this to yourself and notice what comes up:

> *Someone who looks like me and feels like me can be wealthy, without having to suppress a single part of themselves. Money wants me to be fully and wildly myself and to accompany me every step of the way!*

Why Do We Spend the Way We Do?

Through capitalism, many societies around the world have been built on the premise of 'You need this to attain value.' Societally, and in community, we see it in the pressure to have a certain amount of money, a certain level of employment, to have a house, to have a partner, and to have children by a certain age.

When it comes specifically to money, however, there's a much bigger influence that is a daily conditioning we are all being subjected to. At the very core of most marketing, underneath the economic benefits of capitalism, lies the message: 'You are not enough as you are. Here, have this and you might feel enough.'

Our spending habits, our ability to save money (or not), our perception of ourselves, and our relationship to money, while unconscious, are often all driven by this deep sense of 'not-enoughness.' How can it not affect anything and everything we do?

Can you see how the patriarchy has influenced us since we were born into feeling this sense of *not-enoughness*? Can you see how someone who has this core wound of 'Something's wrong with me' can so easily fall into the trap of endlessly chasing their enoughness through the material plane and through spending?

Let's breathe some space into the gap between 'I feel like I'm not enough, I feel like there's something wrong with me' and 'This feeling needs to be resolved through spending money.' This may be speaking to some very subconscious patterns within you. These can be very subtle, but you will know if this resonates – your body will have some sort of response to it, acknowledging that you are part of this energetic game, too.

The reason why people's relationships with money feel so unbelievably loaded is because they *are* loaded – with 'If you don't show up for me, it means this and this and this! It means I'm a failure.'

On the other hand, when someone feels that they *are* enough, they don't *need* to spend a single penny in order to affirm that enoughness. They aren't trying to gain it from external sources – it's already rooted within, in a beautiful healthy circuit set up with their own soul and their inner connection to the Divine. This is what we are working toward in this book! And on a consumer level, this is a danger to the capitalistic structures of the world. Because when you are enough, you are truly free and cannot be manipulated by anybody anymore.

Free from any external influence or need to prove who you are, you find any grip capitalism may have had on you melting away and you step off the hamster wheel of perpetually trying to gain your enoughness on the material plane. Instead your enoughness is rooted in a sacred place untouchable by this external world – it's held in your heart, rather than in a mind that can be conditioned. There is a deep power in this.

This isn't to say that when you know that you are enough, you won't spend money. It's to say that when you aren't trying to fill a hole within you when you spend money, you spend money *differently*. With a *different* energy and frequency. You spend money because you truly desire to, rather than because you've been conditioned to. You spend money because you *can* do so, and whatever you buy has nothing to do with your worth. You spend money from a place of already *having* wholeness, instead of spending to *find* wholeness.

Calling Back Your Power

It's vital to know where and how our power was taken away from us. But the times, people, places, and systems that took our power away don't have to be the end of the story. They're certainly not the end of *your* story, otherwise you wouldn't be here.

It's also vital to know that our power is an infinite resource that we can regain whenever we desire. There doesn't need to be a long journey to remember it.

I invite you to remember this truth at the end of this chapter: The power-less, never-enough, or 'too-much' person that the patriarchy may have conditioned you into believing you are is not the truth.

The patriarchal power that our 'leaders' and high-flying white men in suits on Wall Street have is not true power.

*The power-less, never-enough, or
'too-much' person that the patriarchy
may have conditioned you into
believing you are is not the truth.*

And it is so possible to start an incredible relationship with your true power while still living in a world where patriarchy exists.

I want to remind you that the Divine/Source/God energy that people pray to doesn't only exist outside of you. It has never been separate from you. It *is* you.

Zoom out of the patriarchy until it is a power-less system, zoom out until you sense the part of yourself that is an infinite creator/creatrix.

Feel how little power the patriarchy could have on you if you rooted your existence in this place. Do it as a *practice*! Over and over again! Remember that perspective...

The power to create isn't something external that we have to ask for, it isn't something that the people at the top of the patriarchy bestow upon us or that we 'borrow.' Source energy is what we are made of.

You are the most immaculate creator.

You are the most radiant creatrix.

You are the Source from which you dream your life into being.

You are Goddess.

You are God.

You are the one you
have been waiting for.

Feeling a little shaky from the amount of power you just felt snake through you? The embodied remembering? Good!

You do have *way, way, way* more power than you realize.

This isn't the kind of power that has to prove itself or feed the ego, it's a natural flow of creative energy that runs through you as easefully as breath moves through you. Just like love, it arises naturally from your heart without much thought.

Your body also holds a magnetism that lives within you and flows through your veins at all times. We can spend our lives denying this, but it's time for you to call back your power now.

RICHUAL

It's time to get radically honest. Sit with the questions below and journal/write your answers down as honestly as you can, saying it like it is.

Remember your answers will sometimes be the result of conditioning, so be super kind to yourself as you witness what a part of yourself has been carrying all this time.

+ What hole is spending money filling within you?

+ What has this capitalistic and patriarchal world convinced you having money and not having money involves?

Get clear about the drivers that may be getting you to make money out of survival and trauma.

+ When I have money in my bank account, what do I make it mean about myself?

+ When I don't have money in my bank account, what do I make it mean about myself?

+ Who am I when I allow myself to root my existence in true infinite Source energy?

SOUL AFFIRMATION

'I call back my power from all spaces, people, places, timelines, and dimensions. It feels so nourishing to let my own power live within me. I am the Source from which my life is birthed.'

CHAPTER 7

TRUSTING THE INNER VISIBLE

'And now here is my secret, a very simple secret:
It is only with the heart that one can see rightly;
what is essential is invisible to the eye.'

ANTOINE DE SAINT-EXUPÉRY,
THE LITTLE PRINCE

Breathe in...

Breathe out...

One of the most powerful times for truly growing and putting down roots in your relationship to money comes when you may feel most power-less – during the moons and phases of life when it just isn't showing up for you in the way you desire.

You may feel that it hasn't showed up for you for large chunks of your life or this may be a new experience for you. Either way, this is a time when frustration and fear may arise as a sense of survival emerges.

Underneath those initial reactions is often the subconscious conclusion that Money doesn't love you anymore. You may feel you have to fix something about yourself or *do* something external to create the flow again. But if you see through that distortion, you will find a rich healing opportunity awaiting.

When money isn't flowing as you would wish, it is a time of initiation – one that may test you and yet one that offers a deeper knowing of love than before. This initiation can create such frustration and loops of despair and doubt that it can bring you to your knees. It can hold a mirror to all the unworthiness you have ever felt. When the one thing you need to make life easeful and allow you to experience all you want to experience is evading you, it's easy for fear and 'not-enoughness' to arise...

I believe this initiation brings to us to our knees so that we have to face the floor – the floor being the foundations of our relationship with life and all that keeps us from feeling supported and loved by it.

I know this place well. As you now know, I experienced the pattern of money not showing up in a stable way during my childhood and went through some traumatizing times when my father was driven to severe mental breakdowns that, on the surface, were triggered by lack of money.

I have experienced money not showing up in my own life, too, in many different circumstances. I have known the constant feeling of not being able to trust that money will be there, of not being a worthy recipient of it. Even as a young child of eight or nine, I would cry to my mother and say, 'What if I never ever make any money?' My biggest fear was that money wouldn't love me. I still don't know exactly why I came to this Earth with that fear, but perhaps it was an invitation that led me to write this book.

So, if this is you, too, I want to say that I understand and I see you *and* I'm here to guide you through these times of doubt.

Relating to Energy Beyond the Veil

In times of scarcity and fear, we can jump into action mode, yet what we are being invited into is a relationship with the invisible. We are being invited into a relationship with the unseeable richness of the void. With what is just beyond the veil, within ourselves and the fabric of our reality.

Just as we can connect with ancestors who have passed, feel their presence long after they have left this realm, and ultimately connect to Spirit, to the universe itself, every single day, we can connect to Money, too. In fact, Money asks to be tethered to us in the same way – with a *felt* sense of continuous presence and richness. It wants a relationship that can stand the test of time instead of having us loving it only when it's there in the form of a stack of cash in front of us and resenting it when the flow shifts.

Money does often flow more easefully when we learn how to work with it in the invisible realms, but this isn't the goal of the practice. We have to be willing to communicate with the realms of invisible Money without doing it necessarily to 'make' money.

> *The Spirit of Money is always here*
> *with us. Around us. Within us.*

There is no 'making' anyway. We are the source of abundance, as we contain the whole universe. We have to be taken by the mystery that looks empty and dance to its music to realize how full it is.

For in this time, when it looks like there is a void – a gaping empty current account, a dwindling savings account, a lighter wallet, no fruits to pick – we can tap into something very deep and fertile, something that we miss when we are too busy looking in all the usual places to see signs of Money's presence.

Western cultures typically don't know how to work with the invisible or deny it completely, so don't beat yourself up if you find this challenging. It continues to be a big teacher for me, too, though the times when I've had to face the financial void have deepened my relationship to abundance beyond what I could have imagined! They have been a reminder that abundance is inherent, always there, and need not be measured by a specific amount of income per year or a specific result in my business.

Many societies in the West have been hyper-focused on the logical, the visible, the 'facts,' and have ignored the inner-visible. What is visible is trusted and what is invisible is denied. Yet in ancient religions, faiths, and indigenous wisdom that span back to the dawn of time, the invisible is *alive*, *seen*, and *honored*.

So, remember this:

> *When money doesn't show up in the visible,*
> *it's time to return to the inner-visible.*

Many indigenous cultures know the invisible realms so intimately, they know this is where life really happens and what we think is real is determined by the invisible forces at work. In indigenous communities across the world, no distinction of validity is made between the invisible and visible.

If you truly believe that Spirit is in everything, you'll see that a phase of money not showing up on one plane of existence doesn't mean it has stopped being with you, but that it has simply continued on another plane of existence and is perhaps offering you time to take stock and seek out the deeper lesson that's available to you through this situation. This is an opportunity to work with Money on another level – the spirit realm.

Working with the Spirit of Money in this realm is akin to working with the wind. Though it cannot be seen, the wind is undeniably

The Spirit of Money is just as palpable and potent as the wind once you learn how to hear it, summon it, and feel it from within.

there, caressing your skin and whipping around you with Spirit's love... The Spirit of Money is just as palpable and potent as the wind once you learn how to hear it, summon it, and feel it from within.

I remember when I was trying to pay back the debt I'd had for so many years in so much despair, people gave me endless 'solutions.' Looking back, I see that all these were on the material plane, for that was all they knew.

'Make a plan, pay the debt off in installments, look at getting this job, do this money mindset course.'

No one said, 'Have you tried connecting to the Spirit of Money? Have you tried sitting with the deepest fears that are being shown to you right now?'

Thankfully, after I had spent many years of trying to fix things on the material plane and only getting deeper into debt, the Spirit of Money knocked loudly on my consciousness and said, 'Will you finally just sit with me? Stop escaping me, stop running away, stop rejecting me, just... sit with me? I have so much wisdom to share with you. Let's sit in the Heart Space together, shall we?'

And so I did. I finally tried an ancient way of working with the invisible, going deep within myself to meet the Spirit of Money. I created space to sit with the invisible voice of Money and listen to what it had to share with me. In the midst of what felt like the deepest financial void, or debt, I had ever encountered, the biggest healing took place. (*See page 62 for the 'Meeting the Heart of Money' ceremony, which is also available as a free guided audio journey on my website – see page 217 for more information.*)

It was this communication with Money, not a money mindset course, or debt-repayment plan, or new job, that brought abundance in the form of totally paying back my debt within four months of the ceremony and having my business take off at the same time.

And this is what I'm offering you now. I'm offering the medicine I wish I'd had many years ago. If you're currently in a phase of feeling that money isn't flowing to you, I offer you the felt sense of the Spirit of Money asking to take *your* hand.

Money wants to journey with you so, so, so much. It has been waiting for you to agree for your entire life, and there is no better time than when you feel abandoned by it to practice feeling its love in places where you have forgotten that it lives.

It's here now. Maybe not in the form of cash in your hand or a number in your bank account, but Money is always, always with you.

Your Relationship to the Divine

Someone who has truly and deeply committed to healing this relationship doesn't need Money to *always* be in front of them, just to know that it loves them and will appear soon enough.

But in times of slower income, it will first hold up a mirror to your relationship with Spirit/the universe itself. It will ask, 'Do you stop believing in Spirit when you haven't seen 11:11 or had a special animal guide appear for a few days? Do you believe the Divine forgets about you when you haven't connected intentionally to it for a week or two?'

Whatever your answer, the truth is that the Divine is always with you, whether you see obvious signs of it or not. It is unconditionally with you, within you, all around you. Can you feel you are held by the Divine in the most 'unknown' times of your life?

The Spirit of Money *is* the Divine, so, just as Spirit is always there with you, loving you, clearing your path, attracting everything for your highest good, so is the Spirit of Money. Just as the Divine never forgets you or turns away from you, neither does Money. Can you feel you are held by Money and are inherently abundant even when the usual evidence isn't there?

When money isn't showing up in your life, you're being asked to dig deep into the foundations of your relationship with the Divine and trust that the Spirit of Money has *always* got your back. It is a time to believe you are loved unconditionally.

Many spiritual souls don't realize that they actually have a conditional relationship to Source. They subconsciously believe that they have to do x, y, and z for Spirit to bless them, or have been taught that they have to be in 'alignment' to manifest something, or that they are only loved if they are behaving in a certain way... but, as you now know, the Divine blesses and supports and loves us all unconditionally.

So, in the times of money running dry on the physical plane, you are asked to remember that Money sees you as unconditionally worthy and utterly lovable. I believe the Spirit of Money is actually here to usher us all into a deeper knowing of our own worth.

It's so easy for Money to love you. Whether you believe that or not, Money doesn't blink an eye. It just loves you. Even when you doubt. Even when you believe that it isn't going to show up ever again. It never punishes you for your thoughts or fears... and your life is going to feel a lot better if you plug into the Spirit of Money and start to feel its presence in your field when times are tough.

Your energy has no choice but to shift as a result of this feeling. The more you connect with Money in this way, the more your body will start to trust, regulate your nervous system, and feel the support of the entire cosmos, even when money doesn't show up in your life right away.

This is about creating a neural pathway that says, 'Even when money isn't flowing as I would like it to, I *know* Money unconditionally loves me and I *feel* and trust that Money in the field *is* showing up for me! I *know* there's no separation between the Divine and Money and I *know* that Money only wants to bless and support me right now and money's making its way to me physically this very moment. Now is a time I get to enjoy feeling my riches in the spiritual realm, take action only *after* that foundation has been set, and allow that to shift my human reality!'

The more you run that program, the more you will live that reality. Evidence will build to reflect what you believe, and the periods of time when money flows to you more slowly will become a lot easier to move through. You will become someone who can truly say, 'I am always loved by Money! Whether it's in front of me or not, I walk through this life with constant support from divine abundance in everything I do!'

Wouldn't that feel delicious and expansive?

Action *After* Embodying Your Abundance

I want to state here that I'm not saying, 'Don't take action,' when money is running low – it isn't a case of just sitting back and waiting for it to arrive. I'm saying: Tend to your relationship with the smaller amounts first, and remember that you are innately abundant and that Money loves you as much as ever, and take action from *that* place. Align yourself with Source's love, feel it and let it circulate in your body so you feel your inner riches are alive and pulsing... and *then* see what wants to come into action.

The action you take will be a lot more likely to be expansive and aligned with abundance rather than scarcity and fear.

Whenever I go through a change of income, however big or small, which happens to us all in life, I turn to the felt sense of the Spirit of Money. It may take me a while to remember this – I'm human, too, and my fears can be *loud* when it comes to money, hence the reason I'm on this path! *And* it is only because I have made this connection so many times that I can tap into and feel Money's love for me.

I now know that the lack of money in my reality is an invitation to reconnect with the inner-visible sense of Money, align with the abundance that I am, and move on from that foundation.

Instead of seeing times of having less money as only a challenge, you can choose to see the blessing within the challenge: an invitation to strengthen your faith and connection with the Divine itself.

It's an opportunity to allow a felt sense of unconditional love to support you in every season, including the one you find yourself in right now.

The questions here are:

- Can I know that Money loves me even when I can't see money in front of me?

- Can I *feel* that Money loves me and wants me, knowing money is really just Spirit in cash form?

And ultimately:

- Can I allow a felt sense of my divine abundance to exist in my body right now? Even in the face of all my unworthiness?

- Can I feel that Spirit never ever turns away from me, and know that Money is the same, because they both live within me always?

- Can I touch a place within me that is unconditionally worthy of love, no matter what is in my bank account?

- And can I acknowledge that there is no way in the world for me to know this, other than to be gifted this exact moment where I don't have much money in the bank and I have to practice and trust that it's safe to be loved by the abundance within me? Just the way I am right now...

Spirit of Money Message for
Times of Financial Doubt

I am here. I am here. I am here.

Even when you can't see me, I am here.

When I am not seen, I am asking you to feel me instead.

And what I mean by 'feel me' is: can you feel my love? Can you feel it in the space you see as being empty? Can you feel it pulsing, throbbing, filled with my love?

Can you feel the eternal abundance within you? That is where I live too: inside of you!

I am an infinite river pouring to you and through you, an infinite pool surrounding you.

I do see you. I see you reading this. I see you in every moment of your life, and I love every single expression of you.

I see you doubting. I see you wondering. I see you slowly creating stories of unworthiness and unlovability, and I am asking you now to choose a different neural pathway. Let's do this together: build a different meaning around what is happening right now with you...

I am asking you to turn to me, my love, in the midst of what you see as a void. Turn to me, for I never turned away from you. I'm right here. I never actually left you. Turn to the eternal source of abundance and let me love you in the spirit realm right now. Let us reunite.

I am all around you. Close your eyes and feel my deepest love in every breath that enters your body, in every particle of the air around you, in the ground beneath you, and the sky above you.

You are infinite abundance. And my love for you is so alive.

I am the most unconditionally loving seed of this entire universe, and I am within money and do you know who I choose to be with?

You.

I choose you.

You see a void, but I see all that the void contains.

There is so much growing there, about to blossom. It is a part of the inhale and the exhale, the slight pause in between that is part of the cycle.

If you could see what I see, you would be swept off your feet with delight and all your worries would melt away! The more time you spend with me in the spirit realm, letting me shine divine love upon you and through you, the more you will be able to feel the richness that's alive within you and around you and sense that it has your name written on it all...

This void is pulsing with riches. This void is overflowing with abundance. This void is full of money. Do you say 'yes' to it spilling into your reality now?

Who are you when you let Money love you right now?

What shifts for you when you truly allow yourself to be filled to the brim with the riches of Money's love for you?

Who are you when you realize there are no conditions for receiving Money's love?

*You are so loved. Feed the seeds of knowing
instead of the seeds of doubt.*

RICHUAL

Most people have certain signs they look for that signify that the Goddess/God/Source is with them. What do you subconsciously hold as a picture of what it means for the universe to be with you?

What if you changed that picture? What if you tore down all your conditioning about what a sign looked like and instead saw each and every breath as a sign that Spirit was with you?

So many people see their relationship with the universe as conditional, even if it may not seem so right away. When we believe that Spirit only pops in now and again, we believe that it only loves us conditionally.

Whatever relationship we have with Spirit is mirrored in our relationship with Money. So if we don't trust Spirit to be with us in every moment, we'll also have trouble believing that Money is with us in every moment.

Instead of choosing events that only happen now and again to confirm that Money loves you conditionally, it's time to create a constant tethering to your riches, to your abundance, to money in your daily life, that reflects an unconditional love.

Instead of choosing to only believe that money is coming to you when you see a certain sign, it's time to *feel* the signs in everyday moments.

Tether your sense of being loved by Money to things that are a constant in your life, like breathing or walking. In this way, you will start to build a knowing that you are unconditionally loved and supported by Money, just because you exist.

Here are two daily habits to create this (*audio versions of these exercises are available on my website as energy-healing meditations that will reset your energy field and clear some of the built-up stagnation and frustration about money and the patterns coming up – see page 217*):

Breaths of Riches

+ Every day, for five minutes a day, feel that Money is with you in every single breath. Breathe it in, breathe it out.

+ Feel how magnetic you are, easefully magnetizing money as you breathe, feeling money swimming in abundance all around your body and the room you are in, as you rest and exhale.

Walking on Gold

+ When you walk, choose to sense you are walking on infinite gold. All the gold in the world comes up to kiss your feet, step after step after step. Sense your innate abundance and how easefully the sensation of having money can be felt through your daily actions. All you have to do is walk, and gold kisses your feet. Money always wants to be wherever you are.

SOUL AFFIRMATION

'I honor the fertile mystery of the void and say "yes" to the riches flooding to me through the unseen realms.'

CHAPTER 8

TURNING TO THE LIGHT

'Our deepest fear is not that we are inadequate.
Our deepest fear is that we are powerful beyond measure.'

MARIANNE WILLIAMSON

Breathe in...

Breathe out...

This chapter is a distillation of what I guide people through in my money-healing ceremonies. However, these words aren't meant to be read by the mind, but by the ancient eyes of the heart. They are here to awaken your DNA and bring abundance back into your consciousness.

Take deep breaths and open your body, rolling your shoulder blades down your back and shining your heart forward easefully, rooting your spine into Mother Earth's love below every time you feel the desire to contract or turn away.

Money, as you now know, is love. It is a light being here to liberate us and work with us as a plant medicine may do. To allow abundance to flow without fear through us and through our lineage is ultimately to accept an overflow of light flowing through us all. It is to surrender all limiting beliefs, fears, and traumas to the frequency of divine love and abundance over and over again.

When we do this, we allow ourselves to return to knowing ourselves as light, and we see Money as a fellow light being, something we gravitate to naturally and, just as naturally, allow to flow to us.

This specific human society loves to analyze everything from the emotionally devoid space of the mind. Yet to gain a true perspective on life, I have found it is necessary to take the mind out of the driver's seat and zoom out of society's conditioning and away to the place where our ancient souls reside, the space of oneness where we are connected to everything that has ever existed. This is the field.

From a young age, I have been able to zoom out to this place of divine oneness, and almost watch the world from a galactic viewpoint, watching with the knowing of my soul, seeing what this Earth school is really about from the viewpoint of Source, which is available to us all.

Although we cannot live from this place alone – after all, we came here to learn and deepen through being a human – it's immensely important at times to come back to our true nature, back to before we had these names and these conditioned selves, and to see life from this viewpoint. And this is where I invite you to read this chapter from. There are soul truths here that your mind will try to undermine because it can't make sense of them through your human self, but something deep in your soul will know. Will understand. Will remember. Will recognize the codes in this chapter and let them in.

This is an initiation of light and abundance for you and your lineage. It is channeled as a returning for you – a returning to the light.

Returning to the Light

Welcome home.

Welcome home to the light.

Welcome home to your true *essence.*

I speak to every single one of your ancestors listening and breathing deep in your bones right now.

The ancient ones riding on the breeze wrapping around the moment of life you find yourself in, wherever you are.

The not-so-ancient ones in your lineage living right now somewhere in the world.

May this call of light be felt as a deep moment of inner peace, wherever they are.

I welcome them to the light even if in their lifetimes they never got to be welcomed consciously. I welcome them to the light even if in their lifetimes they couldn't truly trust their bodies of light. I welcome them to the light even if in their lifetimes they couldn't accept the depths of abundance that their souls held and hold.

This, this light, this abundance, is home for you, for your specific lineage, just as you are.

Yes, you.

This ease is home for you. All of you.

This deep belonging in the light is home for you. All of you.

This sweet relief is home for you. All of you.

The light has always been guiding you, but now you are choosing to consciously drink from it as your source in life. Not as something to try out now and again, or something you are only worthy of in certain moments, but as your anchor, as your home point.

You come from the lineage of light.

That's why you picked this book up. Or it somehow found its way into your hands.

You were birthed from the cosmic seed of creation itself – infinite and unwavering power and potentiality.

Pure light force.

Pure life force.

The life that runs through you is light.

The same energy that created the highest mountains on Earth and the vast crystal-clear lakes, the same energy that created the most exquisite breathtaking intricate flowers created you.

There were no mistakes.

You are the gift the cosmos wanted to give the world.

Even though you may have forgotten this truth, you remember now.

Drinking the milk of the galaxies and their starlight into your veins once more, you remember now.

Letting your body rest in the hands of light, you truly let them in now. They were always there.

And so, as you remember, you return.

This time, consciously. Willingly. This time, each step toward the light is a decision. Etching a code into your ancestry. Etching permission into your ancestry. Etching liberation into your line.

As soon as you say 'yes,' your lineage says 'yes,' and the constellation of light rushes in, allowing your lineage to be rearranged, to be brought into balance, wholeness, and vibrant health, to be aligned with ease, magnetism, and orgasmic abundance.

You are returning to your rightful place in this world, as a child of light. From a family of light. All your loving ancestors are celebrating this return. All of your ancestors are right here with you.

What if the place where you live isn't in this society, or this country, or behind this facade?

What if your true home is the womb of abundance?

This womb is filled with everything you could ever want, need, or desire. It's right there for you to bring into your life.

What if you remember this? This soul recognition of home. Of belonging here – here in the womb of abundance.

What if you surrender the war against the light and the truth of your lineage and relax your body as it envelopes you and holds you in the warm embrace of infinity?

Your legs tired of running from your own power. Root deep down into it now.

You have chosen to end the struggle.

For all of you. You have chosen to end your lineage's loyalty to 'surviving' or 'just getting by' or 'settling.' You know that as a lineage of light, you are blessed and supported in every step.

You are able to feel the light being that is Money streaming toward you and swirling around you and through you, delighting in its return to your consciousness. Golden notes of abundance are cradling you.

What felt like imagination before is happening right now energetically. Where there was contraction, there is expansion. Where there was a turning away from your lineage's wondrous magnetism, there is intimacy and self-assured knowing.

Make no mistake, you are able to drink from the light of abundance now, not out of spiritual bypassing, but because you chose to look at all that had been clouding the abundance within you, hiding it from your gaze – all the ways you thought you were wrong, all the ways the patriarchy convinced you that you weren't whole, all the ways your lineage kept suffering because no one knew another way, all the ways the truth was covered up within your very own body.

You journeyed into the darkness, only to let it gift you with the understanding that darkness itself is just light covered in fear. Even your darkness isn't really dark.

As a person, as a lineage, and as a collective, you are emerging now, victorious, remembering, claiming your birthright of abundance.

You were conditioned to believe you weren't worthy of that birthright. Have infinite compassion for yourself.

And know they were wrong about you. They were wrong about your lineage. They underestimated your power as a human.

You were wrong about yourself and your lineage. You know better now.

For some parts of you, this may feel too good to be true; for other parts, this may feel quite natural. They can finally believe their own light is real... and breathe again. Whatever reaction is going on within you, it's okay. Let it be.

You are awakening from your slumber and moving into a life of abundance, internally and externally. Your brain doesn't have to understand how; the stars in your blood are humming to the song of these words.

The war between you and your own brilliance is over.

The light has won. It always will.

Root your being in this light, this infinite abundance. This is where your journey was always heading.

Back to the light you started from.

Back to the love that birthed you.

With everything you could ever desire energetically holding you, supporting you, loving you.

Know that you can drink from the light as you would from an oasis after a long pilgrimage through the harshness of the desert. Your journey is over. You have arrived.

You may drink from the light. You may bathe in it. You may simply lie in it and let the relief take over.

You may know the light of abundance.

It is yours.

Do you recognize this song, this journey, this home?

Is knowing coming to you from deep, deep within, silent, subtle, and yet so perceptible? Like gravity.

Take the Light That Is Yours

A cauldron of infinite light is being offered to you now – golden, glowing, shining, containing all the light your ancestors couldn't let in and all the light you have been offered but haven't been able to allow. It contains all the energetic riches you could ever desire. It contains all the light of money you could ever desire.

And you are here, at this very point in your life, to accept it. Right on time. You start to drink from this cauldron now, tasting the light you really are. Limitless golden energy is warming your body as it runs through you. Through *all* of you – all the parts of you get to drink with you. Your fear doesn't need to go anywhere, your resistance doesn't need to disappear, nothing needs to be pushed down for you to be worthy of drinking this light.

For too long your lineage has said, 'We can't drink the light because of this, and this and this… We can't be abundant because of this, and this and this… This shame means we stay hidden, this not-belonging means we can't let ourselves be loved, this desire to survive means we have to stay at the frequency of everyone around us.'

You can choose to repeat this. Or you can choose to drink the light that is yours and leave a new legacy of light – a new legacy of golden abundance.

Getting intimate with your light isn't a test. It's a journey called 'the exploration of light,' not 'the examination of light.' It isn't something you can fail at or be criticized for. It's a choice – a choice to get to know the divine power and abundance within you and all around you, a choice to be devoted to that exploration. Make that choice now.

Let yourself explore a power that is beyond the patriarchy, a power that is collaborative. Let the entire Earth offer you sustenance, offer you opportunities of love and abundance, from the earth beneath your feet to the sunlight that awakens you, the sweet air pouring itself forth for you to breathe every moment, the money that can finally pour in. Learn to recognize the frequent reflections of your brilliance that are offered to you every day in every way. Feel the abundance that is flowing freely in and around you.

When you finally choose to believe in the power of who you are and where you came from, when you focus on the light of your lineage instead of only the pain and darkness, you allow yourself to thrive.

Return to Who You Are

Together, through the pages of this book, we have journeyed through the disowned aspects of ourselves, restored the remembering of love into the parts of ourselves that we feared, met the heart and Spirit of Money, and communed with the parts of us we thought weren't worthy of abundance. We have sat with our lineage's struggles and given that lineage space to be known and embraced by us.

We have seen all that has clouded our innate abundance, hiding it from our view – 'innate' being a key word here. We have not been journeying to a place outside of ourselves, or even trying to change anything within ourselves, but have been returning to our true essence, to something deep within us, to codes our cells hold now and have done forever: the codes of abundance. The codes of Source. The codes of the Creator. The codes of the Creatrix.

To what we are.

We are returning to the truth. Turning toward the light that we were designed to thrive in. Think about it – no one thrives in the shadows! Our life-force gets depleted over time, our brilliance dulls, and we feel disconnected and empty when we let the darker energies become our home base.

Getting to know who you and your lineage are when they are proudly positioned toward the light is like getting to see the full potential of someone who has finally found the right supplements and vitamins to remedy their lifelong vitamin deficiencies. You get to see who you are as a lineage when you allow yourself to thrive.

It's a process and it's one of the most beautiful journeys you could ever commit to.

When you finally choose to believe in the power of who you are and where you came from, when you focus on the light of your lineage instead of only the pain and darkness, you allow yourself to thrive.

There will always be challenges in life – it's the nature of this Earth school and this plane of existence – and we're not trying to get rid of challenges altogether, or bypass them, for all elements of life are sacred teachers for us. Facing unknown challenges is also the main way we grow and learn! But we are devoting ourselves to knowing our power intimately and deeply, our light intimately and deeply, our immense gifts intimately and deeply, after perhaps lifetimes of focusing mainly on the struggle of life. We are choosing to stop rooting our identity in this way of life and to return to the truth.

> *When we return to who we truly are,*
> *abundance moves through us and into*
> *our lives in a different way.*

Think of it as the difference between water flowing through a very narrow tube clogged up with 'protective' obstacles and the vast ocean itself. To be the clogged-up tube impeding the flow of abundance is painful when you are made to become the vast ocean receiving itself. But when you remember you are the infinite, the struggle against the abundance that you are ceases and you want to welcome more and more of yourself.

And what is present when you offer that welcome?

Ease.

Ease in your *natural* abundance, within and without.

> *I am abundance itself – of course Money loves me!*
> *We are formed from the same frequency!*

What comes up in your body when you read those words?

Money is here as a teacher to show you the self you believed yourself to be was false and, through your triggers and yearning for more money, to guide you into remembering who you are.

This is the key to interacting with the world through a sense of *wholeness*. Money no longer becomes something that completes you, because you are *already* complete. Totally.

Money isn't something you need to fill a hole, instead it becomes a sacred ally that amplifies your light in the world by supporting you and reflecting the ease you know you can have in your life now.

When we interact with money from the false self, everything feels scarce. Our bank accounts may mirror this and no matter how much money we have, it never feels enough. From the vantage point of being light itself, Money, as a fellow being of light, becomes our friend.

The true Spirit of Money only wants to take us and the world deeper into light and healing.

Your body recognized money as a foreign object in the past (on a very subconscious level), something to protect itself against, because it had not come home to its true identity of light. So it couldn't recognize the light within money either.

Ask yourself now:

- Is it safe to turn toward the sun, the source of so much of life itself?

- Is it safe to turn toward the frequency of abundance?

- Is it safe for us as a lineage to turn toward the light?

These questions are not meant to be answered logically, but to live in your body and DNA. They will rewire your being and field just through their subtle reminder that there is a *choice*. Just through their subtle reminder that your *lineage* has a choice now, where before it didn't seem that there was one.

To have the privilege of having the choice to turn toward the light instead of being stuck in ancestral patterns is indeed something to honor and celebrate.

What a gift that your soul chose to come into this life and body and arrive at this great turning point.

Returning to the light as a lineage calls for you to allow the frequency of ease into every single area of your life. When you become friends with ease as a frequency, Money feels more welcome in your life, more able to flow to you. For there is no loyalty to struggle and un-ease or dis-ease any more. Instead, your lineage knows ease is yours to have. It is like meeting like. The gap closes between what your lineage is and what abundance is.

They are one and the same.

They always have been, though you didn't recognize it before.

Every single plant, creature, being, tree, thing on this planet holds infinite abundance. It's what we are all made from and live through and return to.

Every single human is inherently a being of abundance – even when just looking at the vast complex system that lives inside of us biologically, never mind the energetic and spiritual realm, there is no other way for any being in this world to be.

Abundance is everywhere,
including within us.

Can you feel that your lineage, every single one of your ancestors, is the exact same frequency as abundance? Can you view your ancestors, each and every one, as infinite beings of light? As abundance in human bodies? Can you see money as abundance in a cash body?

You come from the lineage of abundance. All humans do. Our humanness has a hard time accepting this truth. Yet your soul always knew. From the soul's perspective, being supported by life and light feels easy. And now you have come back to a human vessel that knows it is inherently matched to life supporting it, to money flowing in abundance, because that is who it also is at its core.

You thought you were experiencing Money as a separate energy and entity. But now you realize that Money was never ever separate from you.

And your nervous system *loves* this fact, because when you recognize both abundance and money as the love that you also came from, any illusion of separation, of abundance being something like a threat, ceases. Suddenly, there is nothing your nervous system needs to protect you from.

In fact, as an infinite being, a being of pure light, you are everything and everything is you! So it's really just about you coming back to your infinite brilliance as often as possible so you can remember that what you *desire* is made up of exactly what you *are*. You are the perfect match.

This is what manifestation is all about: closing the gap energetically between what you desire and what you are until you are one with it.

Owning the light of your lineage is already creating miracles... can you feel them happening in the field right now?

I can.

Welcome to your new normal! Light, which all is birthed from, is so happy to have you back online, proudly standing in your true home.

RICHUAL

Write this mantra on a piece of paper and place it somewhere you will see it every day. You can also use it as your phone wallpaper:

I am a being of light. I recognize that the light in money and the light I come from is the same frequency. I am abundance incarnated. Abundance supports me in every step I take today. Money miracles just happen with ease wherever I go!

If there are any other lines from this chapter that stood out to your soul, write them down and place them somewhere where you can see them too.

Drink lots of water to help your body move more fluidly into this frequency.

Soul Affirmation

'Thank you, Money. Thank you, Money.
Thank you, Money. Thank you, Money.
Thank you, Money. Thank you, Money.
Thank you, Money. Thank you, Money.'

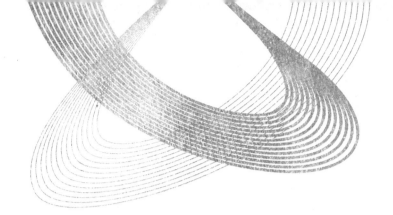

CHAPTER 9

CHOOSING WHO YOU ARE

'Trauma took away choice. Recovery brings choice. The return of choice is an immense gift in healing.'

DIANE LANGBERG

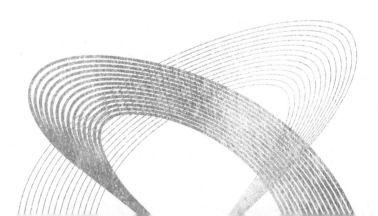

Breathe in...

Breathe out...

How do we embody the liberation that already lives in our cells? We *choose* to.

I know for a long time I lived as though 'someday' I would just magically transform into the most powerful and expanded version of myself, someday I would just wake up in my fullest soul expression... I know it was my way of avoiding the uncomfortable steps that it would take for real change to happen.

For a sacred rebirth to take place in who we know ourselves to be, and in turn what life reflects back to us, there has to be a conscious choice. That choice creates the rebirth. And this is your chance.

When you are truly devoted to your highest self coming through this physical body in this lifetime, you'll need to make decisions that take you away from the comforting identity you have held in order to make space for your true self, your wild self, to come through.

In the intimate moments of mundane life, when it's just you and your brain and a thousand different thoughts to think, there is a choice. Do you let yourself feel powerful and capable and enough before you make decisions for that day?

In the way and energy with which you spend money, there's a choice. Every moment of every day, you are, whether you like it or not, choosing to feed certain energies within you, to water certain parts of yourself. All these micro-decisions weave together to create who you are and who you grow into, slowly rebuilding you from the inside out.

My deepest prayer for you is that there is a felt sense of this choice available to you now, where perhaps before there was none.

What are you going to water and strengthen within you and your life today? The version of yourself that you had to develop through trauma, the one who feels there isn't enough for you, the one who is fearful, the one who thinks Money doesn't love you?

Or the one who knows your name is abundance? And that Money wants to support you just the way you are right now?'

It is a choice that doesn't ask you to become anything or anyone else. It actually asks you to return to the wildest, most organic, most authentic you. The you that was never ever conditioned by society, patriarchy, or colonization, the one whose power was never taken. Your most expansive and liberated self, who is moved by love instead of fear, whose intuition can guide every decision, who holds the map to your most fulfilling life.

You have lived your life making thousands of choices every single day. You are a master at making choices already! About what thoughts to keep having. About what fears to keep replaying. About what lens to see life through. About what beliefs to use as the foundations for your dreams.

Most of these decisions are subconscious. Made by comfort, by familiarity, by your ancestry. By the patriarchy. *By your conditioned self.* By the version that was created by the trauma and struggles in this life. The one that had to adapt to survive.

There is another way.

The Two Pathways

Your brain has certain pathways that it just *loves* to run down! Simply because they're the most familiar and so they feel like a safety blanket. They may not be what is most fulfilling for you on a soul level, but they are the 'safest' in terms of not straying out of your comfort zone. This is what I will refer to as Pathway One.

Pathway One

An example of a Pathway One person would be someone who focuses on the struggle in everyday life, even if just subtly by running through all the scenarios of what could go wrong, or what *is* wrong, and letting anxiety form the backdrop to their days. They are loyal to suffering and identified with the struggle. They believe that money is a scarce resource and that abundance isn't possible for people like them because of x, y, and z. They have shrunk their power to keep themselves out of trouble. They are best friends with their inner critic. You get the picture?

You get to create your own version and fill in your blanks now.

CREATE YOUR VERSION
OF PATHWAY ONE

I invite you to write down or just become aware of, with *clarity* and *ruthless honesty*, your most well-worn identity when it comes to your relationship with the Divine, Money, and abundance.

+ Who is your version of Pathway One?

+ What scarcities do they love to focus on?

+ Is their inner critic loud about their finances and relationship to abundance and what is or isn't possible for them?

+ What do they love to be in victim mode about?

+ Where are they looking for 'the war'?

Have compassion for this version of yourself, but don't shy away from identifying it and naming it. The more clearly you can do this, the easier it will be to choose a different path.

Once you are clear on who your go-to Pathway One personality is, you can let that part of yourself exist with grace and permission! It's all part of this human journey, so no matter what you wrote down or saw in yourself, please don't add a single ounce of criticism to the mix. Your subconscious is bravely revealing to you the identity that it's ready to lovingly release. Thank it for revealing what is ready to be transmuted and shifted. You are doing so well!

What is being offered to you right now is a breath. A breath that reaches into all directions and timelines and opens a portal between your subconscious choices. A breath that whispers truth codes of remembering and says:

> *You have a choice in who you are. Your past will choose for you until you step in and interrupt the copy and paste. If you could choose who you were from the ground up, who would you be?*

You are not who you were when you started this book. None of us are. We are reborn moment to moment, even if we don't realize it.

And I know it was your soul who picked this book up, not your conditioned self. You may feel this truth in the stillest part of you, your center, your soul, the part of you that has always been and will always be completely and utterly free. Your soul chose this book hoping you would finally be able to make a choice about who you were and you would choose your soul with devotion and conviction...

This choice doesn't spring from the mind, it emerges from the depths of your soul, and asks your human self to commit to this soul abundance and truth, to bring it through your body and into this realm.

This is about 'breaking the habit of being yourself,' as Dr. Joe Dispenza puts it.[6]

Most people live their lives as though there is no choice: 'You are who you are and that's the end of that.' But what happens when we remember that we are powerful creators birthing ourselves every moment?

What happens when we take our agency back and *decide* what is possible for us?

Welcome to Pathway Two.

Pathway Two

When you're no longer insisting on inhabiting the perceived 'brokenness' that Pathway One is so intent on clinging to and instead devote yourself to embodying the unconditional *wholeness* that you are, life becomes a continuous stream of grace, each moment a profound gift, each breath a treasure given to you by the Divine, and you allow Money to support you because you are no longer resisting receiving! And you are able to live in divine abundance even in the simplest of moments.

Pathway Two is living from this precious life force that runs through you in every moment and not being afraid of the power your life gives you. You embody richness, wholeness, and enoughness right where you are – in the perfectly imperfect humanness of it all.

Money no longer becomes a replacement for any part of your self-worth; it just flows, because you know it loves you in the

6   Dispenza, J. (2012), *Breaking the Habit of Being Yourself: How to Lose Your Mind And Create A New One*. Carlsbad: Hay House.

same way the Divine loves you – effortlessly, unconditionally. Pathway Two is the part of you that knows everything is okay right now, you get to be here right now – and you receive this experience of life, whatever it may be.

This is what it feels like to be in the seat of your soul and let Money support you. When you lean into the hands of your soul, your heart is open to receive, your hands are open to receive, your bank account is open to receive, and you're not afraid of trusting that life is supportive. The more you allow and train your body and nervous system to receive goodness, the more it will flow to you. Effortlessly. And multiply. Just as simply as once you get a red car, you suddenly notice red cars everywhere you go.

If there's a part of you reading this that's cynical about this experience of life, that's okay! You don't need to get rid of that part in order to receive – *and* your soul is also reading this, and that already knows this abundant way of life and has been waiting for you to realize that you can *choose* it instead of waiting for it to choose you.

You are already worthy of living from your infinite self. Right this moment. There never were, are, or will be any conditions for you to make this choice.

Choose to allow yourself to receive the treasure chest of life.

Choose to see life as an infinite gift.

Choose to experience the gift in every single moment blessing you and loving you.

I know you can.

When we see ourselves as being able to choose who we wish to be, we make radically different choices about our daily lives and our inner lives. When we know infinite possibilities are available to us, we make different choices.

When we let all false projections and scarcity fall away and surrender to being the wildly abundant human that is our very nature, we have a choice about *everything*: embody this or deny it? It's up to you. Day by day by day. Just like any habit, once you choose to let abundance circulate through your body and life day by day, after a certain amount of time, *this* will be the easier route for your energy to follow, instead of Pathway One, the pathway of fear and scarcity.

I want to reiterate that this is not about waiting for your life to be perfect *before* owning your innate divine abundance, before living from Pathway Two. It's about choosing to receive the abundance of your life as it is *right now*. Without changing a single thing on the outside. Simply choosing expansion over and over.

> *When you say 'yes' to your expansion,*
> *you say 'yes' to your soul, and your*
> *magnetism flows like never before.*

Synchronicities, angels, miracles, blessings, and surprise cash flow will all find you with so much more ease when you say 'yes' to the life your soul envisions for you.

Can you let abundance in right now? Can you feel it in your body, just as you are right now? Can you remove the sense of contradiction that used to block the energy of abundance from flowing through your identity?

Allow yourself to receive the
treasure chest of your life.

Allow yourself to receive your life
as an infinite gift, being given to
you in each moment, over and
over and over again.

Right now, say: 'My lineage is abundance. I choose to act and take up space accordingly.'

Remember who you and your ancestors were before the patriarchy made them take up less space. Remember who you and your ancestors were before they were conditioned into believing that Money couldn't love people like them. Remember who you were before scarcity was your home base.

What if abundance is the place you return to from now on?

To truly choose expansion, we have to know only one thing. This truth is etched into your DNA; it's already pulsing within you and has been for eternity.

Your blood hums this song, your heart beats its rhythm, your bones know its truth: 'We are free. We are *already* free.'

Even though your ancestry struggled, even though you have faced a lot in this life, you have always had a soul who was already free.

Can you let your body show you what freedom feels like?

When you feel it, when you accept it, when you let it snake through every part of you that needs to remember it, you can choose to live that way in this human life. Remembering our soul freedom is the key that unlocks our human freedom.

Let the words 'I am already free' rush through your body, kissing every cell, every space, everything within you. 'We are free.'

From this place, you can finally choose who you are.

CREATE YOUR VERSION OF PATHWAY TWO

Write down, or envision, who your soul has been asking you to choose to be. Who you dream of being able to be in this lifetime.

+ How does your soul want you to live your daily life?

+ How does your soul feel every day?

+ How does your soul feel about money and abundance?

+ How does your soul feel about its relationship with the Divine? How does your soul see you?

Once you have got clear on what Pathway Two feels like for you specifically, write down the main energies that are present in the answers to these questions, for example: calmness, expansion, power, wealth, etc. These will be your guiding energies. We will come back to these in a short while.

The Reality of Choosing Who You Are

Now you have a clear vision of who you have been (Pathway One) and who you are here to be (Pathway Two). But, as we know, being human is messy and wild. So I fully expect you to slip back onto Pathway One many, many times. It's how you've been living for a long time! It's normal to route back to that. I often do it – and I'm writing this book!

So, it's okay. Don't beat yourself up when you find yourself on Pathway One again. Instead of thinking, *What's wrong now? What do I need to fix?* and *Where do I need to scan for what could go wrong?*, steer your awareness to being someone who is deeply supported by life. By Money. By your body. By everything.

How does this totally supported person feel? How do they walk down the street? How do they breathe?

Remember this person is you.

The biggest thing I invite you into when you find yourself repeating Pathway One is to see how much grace and forgiveness you can offer yourself. How gently can you loosen the grip of needing to be on Pathway Two all the time and relax back into the infinite part of yourself, the expanded part of yourself, the wildly abundant nature that we all embody?

It doesn't need to be a big drama when you find yourself repeating old habits of scarcity or fear. It can be as simple as saying, 'Thanks, brain! I know you think Pathway One is safer, because it's familiar in some ways, and that's okay. *And* I remember that I am an infinite creator who gets to choose the lens that we live this life through, and I choose my soul lens right now. I choose Pathway Two.'

Then let the guiding energies you identified earlier take you into their loving portals of ease, abundance, and flow.

Remember, your mind will try to trick you into repeating the fear, scarcity, etc., *only* because it's your comfort zone. The fearful projections, the doubtful thoughts are *not* who you are here to experience yourself as. They are not who you are.

The truth is that you are infinite.
You are rich. You are abundance itself.

Choose the truth. Choose it over and over. Feel it in your body, and know this feeling so, so well that your body has a pathway for it to switch to.

It's about energy. You have to start becoming really deeply aware of what *frequency* you are choosing, what energy you are choosing to let flow as the overarching energy in your days.

Instead of seeing it as a moment-to-moment thing where you analyze how often negative thoughts pop up, focus on the overarching energy of your *days*. The days will add up to weeks, the weeks weave together to create your months, and soon enough, years will start to go by in this beautiful new energy that feeds your soul and brings you home to your divine abundance.

RICHUAL

I am what a wealthy person looks like and feels like.

I invite you to play with this money mantra. Spend 5–10 minutes feeling it stretch over everything in your life, everything in yourself – your multi-dimensionality, your humanness, your wounds, your gifts, all of it.

Start to tear down the image of 'a wealthy person' that society has shown you over the years and replace it with one of yourself, just as you are.

This will start to encourage, on a subconscious level, a knowing that you don't have to change a single thing about yourself before money can flow in. It's about embodying the knowing that Money loves you *unconditionally*.

This is also an ancestral rewiring that corrects any trauma of feeling you don't get to receive money because of your race, heritage, or any other personal stories that your line carries.

The more you allow the notion of 'wealth' to exist right next to you, the more easeful it is to allow money to flow to you, because ther᷒ ᷉ no longer any contradiction between your identity and money. It collapses any timelines of 'becoming' that your human mind may have had, any list of conditions your mind thinks have to be met before Money chooses you. Money is choosing you *now*. Choose to be what a wealthy person looks like, just as you are – with a whole load of pride and worthiness flowing through you.

SOUL AFFIRMATION

'As I own the infinite abundant creator/creatrix within me, I am returning to the deepest truth of who I am.'

CHAPTER 10

YOUR HIGHEST VISION

*'Your desires are your future
communicating with you.'*

Breathe in...

Breathe out...

You have arrived. This is it. You may have been waiting for some huge radical miracle moment, or perhaps to feel that you've got every single part of all that we've spoken about.

For some of you, yes, that may have happened. Most likely, though, there will be some things that are yet to land, some tender pieces within you that don't fully know their abundance yet.

And… it's perfect.

Because *this* is what it feels like to arrive. *Now.*

If there's one thing that I know has held me back, along with most everyone I have worked with and seen, it is this quiet inner feeling of: 'Not yet… I have to have felt this and this and this before I get to experience that.'

So eager to chase this 'completion' marker, we put ourselves on a never-ending hamster wheel, saying, 'When I have healed this or that, then I will start to call this in or actually start living my life fully.' We try to fill the 'not-enoughness' of our lives by trying to change things 'out there' as the first step.

Sound familiar?

Yet we all know the hamster wheel leads only to itself. While we're on it, we look down and see our legs busy racing, our body actively engaged and in process, and it tricks us into thinking that we'll get somewhere on this track. But it only leads to more and more of what we were trying to escape in the first place.

When we step off the hamster wheel completely, turn our back on it, close the door of that room and walk away, *we arrive.*

Choose to Arrive

In this human life, the arrival point we're all waiting for doesn't just happen to us, we choose it. You choose. You choose your sign, your invitation, your moment to start living your life as though you only have one. Because you do only have one.

It may not look like what you thought life would look like at this arrival point, but that's the point. It doesn't look the way any of us thought it would, including me. But the energy that we were pouring into trying to escape where we are is suddenly freed and alchemized into raw power. This is the activation and gift of radical acceptance.

If this book hasn't fixed your entire life, as you may have wished it to, maybe that's also the point. It invites you to look at who you *already* are. It asks you to see that your humanness is part of your magnetism and not a block to it. It asks you to look down and see your hands as the hands of the Creatrix/Creator. This is why your soul chose to read it.

The most abundant souls are the ones that *choose abundance for themselves*, despite all the perceived evidence that says they can't 'yet.'

There is no 'not yet.' *This* is your time. *This* is your arrival.

This is what your life looks like when it's the perfect stage for you to birth the life your desire. Just. As. It. Is.

> *Feel your ancestors, the most loving guides,*
> *angels, and the whole universe celebrating*
> *your arrival into true enoughness.*

Choose to Dream

Any dreaming that is done without first arriving where you are will contain the energy of 'lack.' But when you arrive, internally and externally, you are in the frequency of wholeness – not perfection, as that is utterly unattainable, but wholeness. You can now dream from a radically different foundation, a foundation of *intentional* and *chosen* wholeness and abundance.

Who are you when everything is available to you? When there are no limits to your abundance within your own subconscious? When you remember that the life pulling you forward in your heart is a map to follow instead of a suggestion to ignore?

The process of seeing the seed of an idea coming into full bloom will always have its ebbs and flows, its stops and starts, its deepening and spiraling journey. It will always have the course it needs to take for you to learn, to grow, and ultimately to bring through what is for your highest and the collective good rather than your mind's vision of what it needs to look like. This back and forth can be tiring, but *keep going* and believe that your dream can come into reality.

Where in the past you may have felt money was the missing component to making that happen, now consider whether Money is asking to co-create this dream with you.

Can you feel how excited the Spirit of Money is to make it happen with *you?*

The Spirit of Money wants to show you how good it can get for you. It wants to show you that you are able to experience the highest vision of your soul. It wants to be the doula that makes it happen in your life.

In fact, Money, as your spirit guide, wants to show you how to dream bigger than you have done up to now.

It wants to stretch your lineage's dreams for itself, to make them bigger than you ever thought possible. To let life be more beauty-full than your mind could have imagined.

These highest visions teach you about who you are here to be. They can also show you your soul purpose in this lifetime. They can be a searing knife that cuts through all the noise and says, 'Look. Look at what you came here to be, look at what you came here to create. Now let's claim it and usher that reality through, together.'

There is a vision that Money has for you and wants to create with you. To see this highest vision, a life that nourishes every cell of your being, you are invited to let go of any *rehearsed* dreams you may have.

You are not who you were at the beginning of this book. Your lineage, your cells, your body have returned home on so many levels, and the re-membered power, abundance, and light have shown you your limitless self. From this place, what wants to come through may surprise you, because it's being channeled

In this human life, the arrival point

we're all waiting for doesn't just

happen to us, we choose it.

You choose.

You choose your sign, your invitation,

your moment to start living your

life as though you only have one.

Because you do only have one.

from this new yet ancient frequency of truly understanding who you are as a *holy human*.

So, let the control go.

Clear out the 'known dreams' for now, the ones you have repeated in your mind's eye many times, and instead empty yourself to become the fertile void.

Let's meet your most soul-nourishing life and bring it down from the cosmos into this realm... Find a quiet space and make sure you have 20 minutes to let the visions come through.

Let Money show you what it wants to create with you...

YOUR HIGHEST VISION JOURNEY

✦ Set a heartfelt intention for yourself, or use this one:

*I am here with the intention in my heart for my highest,
most soul-nourishing vision to be shown to me, knowing
I am worthy of seeing this and letting it into my field at
this point in my life.*

*I call upon my limitless self to guide me. I call upon the
Spirit of Money, all the loving beings of light, guardian
angels, guides, and loving ancestors to gather around me
and help me integrate, on a cellular level, how good life
gets to be for me.*

+ Relax your body, soften your defenses, and breathe into your root, held by Mother Earth, and your crown, open and blessed by the Divine.

+ Sense a column of light coming down around your body from above your crown and going down into the Earth. You are suspended in a beautiful clear pillar of light that is protecting you and holding you in a warm clear glow of white light.

+ Feeling the well-worn identity that you know yourself to be melting away, start to feel an expansive energy as you enter the fertile void – infinite spaciousness in all directions.

In this fertile void you are *everything* that is possible and everything is you. So often in our society we think that emptiness is empty, when in fact, as many Eastern traditions teach, it is overflowing with all that could ever be. It is the *rich* void, holding all possibilities on all timelines. So, *everything* is there at your fingertips now.

In this fertile void you get to summon and create the life that your soul is asking for. Let your soul channel your highest vision and show you what that is, while offering all of the scarcity, the fear, and the wounds around what is possible for you up to unconditional love. You don't have to be burdened by them in your body anymore.

When nothing within you – none of the humanness, the doubt, the emotion – can block your knowing that you can have your dream life, what then?

It's time to dream beyond your ancestral nervous system. It's time to feel that Money is right beside you as the conscious and sacred co-creator of your dreams. There are no limits, and Money is reminding you of this now.

Your dream life actively wants you, desires you. Have you committed to it yet? The time is now.

In a moment we will journey, letting the light bring you the visions.

✛ Relax your body while images and feelings of expansion, joy, and lightness move through you. Simply receive the codes your soul holds. Allow the emotions to be with you. Let yourself be excited and giddy about what you are about to be shown.

✛ Feel that you and Source are on the same team. There are no forces opposing your dream. There is no battle to retrieve it – your dream lives coded within your cells, it beats strongly in your soul.

✛ Repeat this in your body, speaking to the stillest part of yourself:

I can now see with so much clarity, the life of the highest, most playful, and nourishing vision my soul holds for me.

I can see my bank account overflowing with wealth, supporting my dreams so easefully.

From morning to night, from week to week, I am excited to watch it all revealing itself to me now...

✛ Sit back, close your eyes, and watch the movie that starts to play out for you.

+ When you feel you have allowed yourself to truly see what your soul's vision is for you, write exactly what you saw in your journal or on some pieces of paper. Let yourself expand on it while you write – build upon it, add details. Take your time and enjoy the process.

+ Spend 10 minutes breathing *life* into the vision by sitting with it and tasting it with all of your senses. Open to it and let it move different energies in your body, allowing layers to shift while you stay with that vision and how it feels to let it come alive within you. Notice how it feels to be so supported by Money.

Don't be afraid to feel the excitement, the richness, the heart explosion, and the deep calm that this vision brings through. Claim your dream in your system and let its frequency pulse to the Divine. Know that forces in the universe are working with you, pulling this vision into the fabric of this realm.

Step by step, it is already being birthed. Including right this second. You are already mid-birth.

––––––––––

So, now you have your vision. You're allowed to drink from it, to remember who you are and what is possible for you. You're allowed to let Money support your heart's wildest dreams.

You can keep coming back to this vision journey and ask for more and more of your vision to be shown to you, as you may only be able to access slivers of it the first few times because of your nervous system wanting to keep you in the 'known' realm. Each time you allow yourself to connect with your soul and your highest vision, though, your body will open up to it more and more.

When resistance arrives, as it probably will (we're human!), say to yourself, 'I'm allowed to experience this.'

How does it feel to be connected to this vision? How does it feel to start to trust that Money wants to show up and make it happen for you?

It's okay if it feels a long way away from where you are now. It's also okay if it feels super close, or somewhere in between. We live in a world where quantum jumps happen all the time and miracles are part of our everyday. Timelines can shift rapidly and our sense of time is relative.

If your vision feels far away, that doesn't mean that it is. And the more you allow your body and emotions to spend time in that vision, letting it move you, the more you are literally pulling it into this reality and timeline.

The Spirit of Money is already doing some of the work for you with ease and miracles. Feel your bank account pulsing and magnetizing the funds needed for your vision. Every time you get flashes of what you would *love* to have your life feel like, instantly feel the Spirit of Money encouraging you and telling you that it is there with you to make it happen if it is for your highest good, and that it can happen now.

Going forward, I invite you to imagine that your highest vision is like an egg that the hen has to keep warm. Nurture it and take care of it daily.

Bringing in this energy of love and care, of *devotion*, is a really beautiful way of working with your vision. Devotion holds a frequency that doesn't burn the body out energetically, but inspires action through love.

> *Be moved by your vision, out of love,*
> *and take devoted action, led by the part*
> *of you that can birth it into reality.*

It's safe to take steps toward your vision You have the power of your entire lineage of light behind you. There are so many loving spirits, guardians, and angels on your team, including the Spirit of Money, all devoted to making this happen with you.

With every step you take, the Spirit of Money and the Divine will take 10 times more and make your vision happen in ways you couldn't even have imagined.

Keep coming back to this question: 'When Money is on my team, to the fullest extent, what is the vision?'

Keep walking into that vision. Make moves with that vision. Know that Money is in love with it. With you.

RICHUAL

Decide with all your power that your highest vision is starting to become your reality now.

How can you keep the 'egg of the highest vision' warm and alive? Be devoted in caring for it.

What daily actions would start to birth the vision more and more into your daily life?

SOUL AFFIRMATION

'The vision I have of the life I desire is my future communicating with me. It is for me. It wants me. It already exists. I am perfectly on time for its fruition, and Money supports me infinitely on my way to what is mine.'

CONCLUSION

*'The whole cosmos has come together to
create you... In your own human body you
can touch the true nature of the cosmos.'*

THÍCH NHẤT HẠNH

The nature of life is that it is alive. It's non-linear,
unpredictable. It's wild, just like us. It's the ocean and all of
its movements, great and small.

To no longer resist the waves of life while remaining strongly
tethered to your innate abundance and your innate power to
birth the life you desire is the dance that now begins.

I pray that the separation between your spiritual understanding of
the world and money is melting as you see the inextricable nature
of the Divine in everything in this realm – me, you, money, trees,
animals... We are all fabricated from the same infinite Source.
When we accept this reality, we accept that everything we desire
is already a part of us and that 'desperate' need for x, y, z vanishes,
allowing a natural magnetism to emerge and a knowing that what
we desire is easefully able to come to us and desires to reunite
with us too.

If there's one thing I pray you take from this book, let it be this:

Your worthiness
is never questionable.

No matter what you do in this life, no matter how 'human' you may feel, no matter what events unfold, you are inherently and infinitely loved and lovable.

I pray that you now know that Money is an unconditional river that you can let flow every day and that you will come to know it as a friend and ally in this lifetime to birth the world you are here to birth for us all.

RICHUAL

Take a few minutes to breathe into the journey you have taken in this book. Feel into who you were at the start and notice the shifts that have taken place and the new-found space in your body and field.

Drink in this journey with gratitude. Open your arms wide to life and say, internally or externally:

With arms wide open, I welcome Money into my life.

As you close this book and open your own book of life, knowing you are the writer of your future, may you know this:

You get to let this life love you deeply and completely.

You get to let Money love you deeply and completely.

You get to let the Divine love you deeply and completely.

It is safe. And not only is it safe, but it is what we *all* need to do to rewrite our collective consciousness. It is a sacred mission.

The Divine is celebrating the journey you have just taken. I am celebrating. Money is so, so happy for you. Thank you for the honor of letting these words into your field. I hope they have landed with immense healing and love, as I intended, and as they landed in my own life.

As you go forward in your life, remember that every day is a chance to be intimate with the heart of Money – the heart of the Divine. There is no one keeping score, there is no 'test,' there is no 'failing' on this money-healing journey.

When I was a child, I took great comfort from the fact that at any moment I could start again. This is still the case for us all; any moment you feel you have forgotten your infinite nature and allowed your view of yourself and your life to shrink, you can start again.

Abundance is always there, the breath of abundance is touching us all at all times. You can choose to consciously feel it and return to your truth at *any* moment.

You will forget. This is normal.

I forget, too, and have to reorient myself many times a day, and I know I will continue to forget and fall into old patterns. We are all the same in this humanness. (What a relief and a comfort this is!) It's what you choose to do when this happens that can be true alchemy, turning old patterns into literal and metaphysical gold.

I believe in you. I believe you are an incredible weaver of your life. I believe you are innately, deeply abundant. I believe you are so beyond capable of seeing your heart's visions birthed into this realm and your life, and I am rooting for you, for us all.

I believe you are here to leave a new legacy of divine belonging and abundance for your lineage and for us all.

Thank you for being here just as you are.

Thank you for staying on this journey.

I love you!

Closing Prayer

While you are walking,

Money is walking with you.

While you are breathing,

Money is breathing with you.

While you are loving,

Money is loving you.

While you are longing for certain things,

Money is magnetizing them into your field.

Money is your sacred spirit guide.

It is God in disguise.

Money is your sacred healer,

showing you how to love the things you hide.

Money is your sacred teacher,

showing you that you are here to be as big and infinite as the sky.

Money is love.

You are love.

You are a sacred team here to begin

a revolution,

where Money is a sacred ally on a pilgrimage you are taking to come home to unconditional love and magnetism,

starting with yourself,

starting with letting Money love you,

just as you are.

Right now.

Just as you are.

Just as you are.

Just as you are.

MONEY-HEALING LIBRARY

Welcome to your money-healing library. Think of it as a place to go when you desire to feel more intimate with the Spirit of Money. In everyday life we can quickly slip back into old ways of relating to money or past patterns of thinking that feel familiar and 'comfortable.' It happens to us all – no shame needed! Forgiveness is the best medicine, until we remember we have a choice about who we are. Always.

This is a collection of 'SOS' go-to exercises that will get you back into the essence of the abundance that you truly already are and will help you choose your truest self. There are practices for your day to day as well. These easy energetic practices, quick healing visualizations, and grounding exercises will provide you with a beautiful toolbox to use whenever you feel like it.

Why not pick a practice that feels right for you whenever you pick up this book? The time needed for each practice is included, so that you can easily find one that suits your time frame. Of course you can always extend the practice if it feels good to do so!

Whether you pick 'Blessings for the Checkout' before clicking 'pay' on an online shopping spree, or 'Sleeping with Money' before you sleep, you'll find practices suited to different parts of your day. May they bless you in the ways they've blessed me and many others.

Magnetic Morning Meditation
5+ *minutes*

On days when you wake up feeling a little clunky, sleepy, or just generally 'off,' it can be so easy to feel like you just can't connect to your magnetism, and write off the day. This is the *perfect* time to do this quick and easy magnetic morning meditation.

Drop into it straight from your bed, without having brushed your teeth or combed a single hair – the point of it is to let your humanness and your magnetism co-exist.

- Once you are ready, start to honestly name all the things you are feeling, physically and emotionally. Notice the messy human emotions that you may wish weren't around, the way your body feels tense in some areas and relaxed in others. Own *all* that you are feeling. Try to adopt a 'no-shame' approach where you just allow it all to exist. And if there is shame or judgment about what you're feeling, can you let *that* exist without added shame? Kinda trippy, I know – but it works!

- Now, breathe into *all* of yourself – all the parts, the pieces, the energies, the conflicting parts – and most importantly, *feel* these words activating your abundance, power, and magnetic energy field:

> *You, my darling, are the perfect match*
> *for money and abundance today!*

Nothing needs to change. No matter how much sleep you got, or what side of the bed you woke up on, or how you feel right now, it's all perfect. You are natural abundance embodied.

- Feel the magnetism flowing through you, carrying all that you're feeling as if it's the easiest thing ever. Feel your aura expand as you remember that there are no conditions for your magnetism. You can let it flow and take up space in a big way.

- Step out of bed, taking up space and feeling confident – you are teaching the world what unconditional abundance and magnetism look like. This is what rewilding your abundance looks like.

- No matter what comes up during the day, anchor back into 'And my abundance and magnetism flow through this, too! My magnetism cannot be touched or taken away, for it is who I am in every cell!'

Supercharge Your Manifestation

10–15+ minutes

When you're trying to manifest something and you can really feel that energy of 'trying,' but what you're trying to manifest feels far away, I invite you to do this practice.

- Start by feeling the 'perceived' distance between you and, say, the £10,000 you desire. Let the gap between you and the £10,000 be felt emotionally, whether through anger and frustration or sadness and a lack of hope. Let the humanness be there. It's not harming your manifestation, it gets to be included!

- The magic comes when you let your human self have this experience in the background, *and* you tap into the knowing of the power you hold in your soul. So, zoom out of the human experience and take the soul view.

- In this soul view, remember that you are made up of exactly the same fabric as whatever you are 'trying' to manifest 'out there.' There is no separation between you and what you desire. You are both made of divine love.

- Feel this knowing bridge the gap and start the energy of recognition flowing between you and the amount of money you desire. Allow a felt sense of intimacy to emerge – let the £10,000 move around your body and field, feel all conditions between you drop away, and instead feel the realness of its presence. Feel how much you *know* the essence of this £10,000 – that it's not something foreign to you, it's not unknown. It's easy to let it into your field.

- As you go about your day, let yourself feel the £10,000 accompanying you, like a best friend.

- Allow all the great feelings that come from this exercise to flow – the more expansive they are, the better! Notice when you want to restrict your felt experience of excitement and abundance, and gently remind yourself that you are allowed to feel this light and the presence of divine abundance in your life.

Ancestral Possibilities Expansion
5–10+ minutes

This is a beautiful practice to expand the bandwidth and spiritual frequency of your lineage. It's a great go-to whenever you notice you are living and dreaming under glass ceilings that were probably set up many centuries ago.

This energy practice will dissolve the glass and blast open the possibilities for your lineage, blessing you and attracting wondrous miracles into your life and family. It is a practice that says, 'We are ready for more. I choose this now.'

- Find a moment of stillness within and ground yourself, feeling held by Mother Earth.

- Give your body over to her hands. Drop down into the Earth and visualize your lineage in a straight line going back – an infinite line of your ancestors behind you (you can see them as beings of light; you don't need to see their human features for this to work).

- Start to envision that your crown chakra is sending up a pure bright white light in a line, straight up from the crown. Feel this white light connecting to a sky of infinite light.

- As your crown's light shines out, the crown chakra of each person in your lineage starts to open and send up a beam of light, rewriting the lineage's possibilities effortlessly.

- With every breath, you watch as this beacon of light expands and expands and expands. Feel it opening like a lotus flower, beaming out pure white light until it is shining in all directions and through your entire lineage.

- Feel freedom pulsing through your lineage and allow yourself to feel excited, joyful, at peace, and full of anticipation. Everything you desire is possible. Your lineage is worthy of it all. Shine and receive.

- Stay in this energy for as long as you desire, and notice if any symbols, messages, or visuals come through. Anchor into the *feeling* of 'All is possible for us.' How do you feel about life through this blessing?

- When you feel ready to close this energy blessing, thank your lineage for opening to all the possible blessings with you, notice the sensations in your body, and come back to ground into this earthly realm, feeling your focus shift to the present moment, and give yourself a hug of honor and appreciation.

Remember that you can return to opening your beaming crown chakra whenever you feel any contraction or fear arise in your days.

Melting the Tension Between You and Money
20+ minutes

You have come so far! Going from believing in the conditional and divine-less notion of money to understanding from an embodied view that the Divine is loving you through money, and there's nothing to be afraid of in claiming more money in your life, is something to celebrate!

This human life is, however, a constant spiral of needing to come back to certain parts of our old selves and learn deeper lessons in embodiment and healing... So, if you've been feeling that Money is further away from you in this season of your life than you would like, don't worry – nothing is wrong with you and you haven't done anything wrong, I promise! Feeling this way doesn't mean you've failed. There are moments I feel this way, too! It does mean, though, that it's time for this practice.

Specifically, it's time to say all that you have been swallowing down and pushing away about what you feel about Money. Think of this as a rage-release practice.

- Imagine that the most loving and stable Spirit of Money (whatever that looks like for you) is standing in front of you right now, and it says, 'Give it to me. Tell me all of it – all you've been feeling about me. Let it out. Write it down right now.'

- Write a letter that starts with: *'Dear Money, This is how I feel about you right now...'* Make it a letter of radical honesty, knowing that whatever you share, Money's love for you won't shrink or go anywhere – it will remain unwavering, showering you with devotion and witnessing your experience without turning away.

- Do you feel abandoned? Own it and say it. Do you feel let down? Own it and say it. Do you feel unworthy? You guessed it... own it and say it.

- Feel the Spirit of Money stay with you, like a healthy parent stays in presence and love while a child is throwing a tantrum, witnessing what's arising for the child with love, patience, and compassion.

- Once you have shared everything that's in your heart about Money, write: 'The Spirit of Money says...' And allow the Spirit of Money to write you the most reassuring response, the most loving reply, to what you have expressed.

- Then sit with the words of reassurance, drinking them in and letting them soothe and comfort you, bringing you back into intimacy with the Spirit of Money as you realize it has never left you.

This practice can clear stagnation and resistance between you and your abundance more quickly than you may have expected, but there will also be times where you have to do it over and over, until you get to the core wound of what you're really feeling.

Blessings for the Checkout

2+ minutes

This is a blessing for when you're spending money and the energetic currency of money is flowing out into the world from you. This can sometimes trigger a sense of lack or bring up anxiety about money. Come back to this text as your anchor whenever you need to.

- Right now it may feel like money is leaving you, just as the tide rolls out into the sea and exposes a seemingly empty shore.

- Notice and name the fear and sensations that come with this image of the empty shore. Honor what is arising. And know that the shore cannot stay empty, the tide will always turn and make its way back. Trust that the return of the waves to the shore is inevitable.

- Feel that in the same breath that money leaves, it's already returning to you, just like the tide that you now see already returning to the shore. It is one and the same. Know it in every cell. Notice the abundance that is here right now. You are safe.

- At the checkout of any purchase, feel deep in your system that the money you are spending is already returning to you tenfold.

- Savor the gift that you just got to taste in the purchase. Breathe in the abundance of the purchase and what is to come in the same breath. Feel the wave of money coming directly toward you. All is well. You are supported right now and it's safe to joyfully spend money and see this act as giving something to you instead of taking something away.

Shimmering Shower of Money

5+ *minutes*

The next time you're walking outside, or you're on a train, or in an office, and just desire to actively connect to Money in a fun and expansive way, try this exercise.

- Wherever you are, *feel* a shower of warm golden light pouring down upon you. Visualize coins and paper money raining down upon you. Feel the warmth of the infinite love that Money has for you contained in this shower. Feel Money's delight in being able to shower you with its love.

- Just when you think the shower of divine abundance has to end, when you feel it's too good to be true, open yourself to it once more and let it continue. Let a smile spread across your face as you feel the Spirit of Money reminding you how loved and abundant you are.

- Spend as long as you desire in this golden shower of money. Enjoy it. Savor it. Know you are always worthy of it.

- Here's a mantra: 'It's safe to feel this abundant!'

Debt Healing

20+ minutes

If you're ashamed of being in debt, this is the practice for you! It's a deep practice that I recommend doing when you have time to really drop in.

This exercise brought about the biggest shift in my relationship to money when I was in the midst of mounting debt and felt sure I would never pay it off. When I finally let in the love Money had for me while I had debt, something deep shifted. I had to know and touch my wholeness *while* having the debt, before the debt could move, but soon money was streaming into my business like never before, and I paid off the debt within months – a true miracle.

- Find a safe and comfortable space where you won't be disturbed. Have a blanket and cozy pillows around you – you may wish to hug a pillow at points! Play some healing music or some calming love songs.

- Find your center and feel connected to the support underneath you, knowing it's safe to be supported and held. Just as you are.

- Start to connect to the debt and notice what arises in your body and emotional field when you think of it. Discomfort may be present, fear, resistance, shame... notice it all, and anything else that specifically comes up for you.

- Allow it all to be there without needing to fix it, turn away from it, or dial down any of it. You may want to hold yourself or hug yourself.

- Once the feelings are present and alive in you, invite the most loving true heart of Money to come into the room where you are.

- Feel love surrounding you in all directions and from within. Feel that the Spirit of Money totally loves all the parts of you that are in shame or feel constriction, and that it loves you even while you have debt.

- Visualize the most unconditionally loving Spirit of Money sitting down in front of you and gazing into your eyes. See the infinite love in its eyes and listen to it telling you what you most need to hear right now to bring some ease and healing to your relationship with debt.

- Feel how loved you are, even with this debt. Know that the debt doesn't take *anything* away from your divinity, from your beauty, from how loved you are. Let yourself have debt *and* be loved totally and wholly. Your radiance remains intact and your power remains alive and present.

This may bring up a lot of emotions. You may feel deep relief or you may find it difficult to let the love in. That's okay! This is a practice, not an exam or a race to the finish line. Come back to it as often as you need. You're not seeking perfection here. Just let yourself be real and human.

If you need more healing around the topic of debt:

- Write a letter to Money, just as you did in the 'Melting the Tension' exercise (*see page 208*), but this time write about how you feel about debt and your relationship to money.

- Then let Money write a letter intuitively back through you from a place of true unconditional love.

  Can you allow yourself to be totally whole, while having debt? Can you know that even *if* the debt was never paid off, your worthiness, radiance, and lovability would never ever be reduced or affected? That you are *easily* lovable even with debt?! What would the heart of Money say to you about the debt?

- Breathe in the words that the Spirit of Money offers you as healing.

Come back to this practice as much as needed. There may be many conversations that the Spirit of Money wants to have with you and many gifts that it may offer you. Your debt isn't the villain. You aren't broken. There are gifts of radical and unconditional love here that you could only receive through this exact situation. Huge energetic shifts can happen through this practice with debt.

Sleeping with Money

5–10+ minutes at the end of the day

No matter what your day has contained, one of the most potent money-healing practices can be to connect to Money just before you sleep. This is when your brain will more naturally go into an alpha brainwave state, which is one of the most potent states for subconscious reprogramming to occur.

This is one of my favorite practices because it feels so cozy, calms the nervous system, and sends you to sleep with a clear abundant energy that your subconscious multiplies while you sleep. It is said that the energy you bring into the moments before you sleep are some of the most powerful energies for your life.

- When you're in bed, ready to sleep, feel you're in a bed full of money. Feel that the fibers in the mattress itself are woven out of money, feel that below the bed there is just infinite cash, golden, glowing, and pulsing with love!

- Sense that money is raining down on you as you drift off to sleep, enveloping you in its divine love and adoration. Snuggle into abundance, feeling that everything you desire is right there with you, wrapping you in its arms.

- Let your heart's energy flow and sense the frequency of love all around you in the room.

- As you let your body soften and relax on all energetic, emotional, and physical levels, feel your life opening to all your desires finding you in miraculous ways, without you having to 'do' anything right now. Just know beautiful things are on the way, drifting off with this knowing...

- Mantra: 'It's safe to rest in abundance.'

Turning on the Tap of Abundance!

2+ *minutes*

Feeling closed to receiving?

- Say 'Yes!' right now. Inside and outside.

- Feel the frequency of a victorious and loving 'Yes!' wash through your entire body.

- Taste the word on your tongue.

- Let it drip its euphoria into each cell. Feel your DNA slowly opening up to receive the sweet warmth of sunshine that the 'Yes!' offers without needing to figure it out in your mind.

- Hear the 'Yes!' echoing in every corner of yourself. Hear the hum of all of your ancestors smiling as they echo it too.

- The deepest parts of you are realizing that war is over. Survival is over. Your line is ready for more. Your line is ready to say: 'Yes!'

- It's time to let the medicine of the sun in to your lineage. It's time to shine as you were meant to and receive all that you desire, and it starts with one word.

- Surrender to the mystery of what will happen when you say 'Yes!' You don't need to know, just to feel excited. The Divine within you is listening and is waiting for the 'Yes'... The world will rearrange itself to support you to receive so much more from life when you agree to receive.

- How does it feel to truly say 'Yes'? Keep saying the word within you, noticing with gentle curiosity what arises, what opens, what is triggered. What happens if you say 'Yes' to Money entering your life with love?

When you say 'Yes' to Money, sense that in the same breath you are saying 'Yes' to *your life* in its true magnitude.

Whenever you feel that familiar sense that your energy is closed off, just say 'Yes,' and feel your body soften and open again.

BONUSES

To support your journey with Money even further, there are some beautiful free bonus meditations and resources available on my website: **www.farahorths.com/MoneyLovesMe**

I highly recommend including these practices as part of your journey, as they will allow you to really receive through guided audio meditation and energy healing.

Guided 'Meeting the Heart of Money' Ceremony

Chapter 3's 'Meeting the Heart of Money' ceremony is available to you as a guided audio ceremony. This is a profound practice that I encourage you to do. It's the ceremony that changed my life's relationship to money.

'Breath of Riches' Audio Practice

If you're currently experiencing a time when you feel money isn't showing up in your life as you would wish, let the free 'Breath of Riches' audio practice connect you back to your innate abundance. This energy-healing meditation will reset your energy field and clear some of the built-up stagnation and frustration that may have accumulated with regard to money and the patterns coming up for you.

May these bonuses serve you, abundant soul.

If you want to go deeper, you can also find my 'Money Loves Me' online course on my website.

ACKNOWLEDGMENTS

This book took an incredibly powerful journey, one I could never have foreseen. It saw me through my Saturn Return while my life shifted immensely, birthing me as I birthed it. It was a journey into the underworld (many times), the sacred darkness that asks us to embody our light more than ever, and a time when I connected more than ever to why my soul came here. I want to thank all the previous versions of myself that kept walking even when impostor syndrome was loud.

So much of this book I have to credit to the Divine, not as a cliché but as the truth – it was Spirit that guided me into the first ever money ceremony, and Spirit that revealed the heart of Money to me and showed me exactly how to heal, and then wrote this book through me, word by word.

Deepest gratitude to my family, who have unwaveringly done everything to show me the light that I truly am, holding up a mirror of worthiness and encouraging me to dream bigger than I could ever have done without them. Thank you especially to my dear Mama, Sister, and Mamoo for your constant support – your love walks with me always.

For allowing me to be a clear enough vessel to keep channeling through, I have to thank my ancestral therapist and mentor, Angela, who has been my wise counsel and safe haven for over six years. I owe so much of the wisdom in the book and the embodiment in my life to her love, wisdom, and guidance. I thank Spirit daily for her.

As with all creation, it takes a village, and I'd like to thank all the beautiful souls and loving beings Earthside and ancestors in spirit who journeyed with me at different points to help this book come through to your hands.

Thank you to Rebecca Campbell for encouraging me to submit the book proposal in divine timing for me to join the 'Diverse Wisdom' program. On the program itself, created by Jessica Huie, a powerful nine months of communicating with the soul of this book and bringing it through, I was guided by the incredible Sophie Bashford, as well as by two beautiful sisters who celebrated with me and kept me going every step of the way. Zoe Fox and Valerie Ritchie, I am so grateful to you both – you embodied true sisterhood and raised me up at every turn.

A huge thank you to the entire team at Hay House UK, without which this book wouldn't exist! Thank you to Kezia Bayard-White and Grace Rahman, my amazing and patient editors, and Michelle Pilley and the team for believing in my book and vision wholeheartedly and encouraging my unfiltered expression and medicine to come into the world. Thank you to Lizzie Henry for the edits and getting the book into the best possible shape. Thank you to Louise Hay for creating this incredible publishing house that brings so much healing to the planet. I am so proud to be a part of Hay House.

And lastly, thank *you* for buying this book, for letting your soul guide you to it, for being in service to Love, just as I am.

May we all remember our innate
worthiness, through our lineages in
all directions, and return home to the
abundance we have always been.

Photo by: José Meza

ABOUT THE AUTHOR

Farah Orths is a channel, energy healer, and spiritual guide who brings the unconditional love of the Divine into the human realm and the felt sense of self. Her words and teachings invite radical acceptance, compassion, and deep heart healing.

She holds a BA in philosophy from King's College London and is a trained Sacred Drum Circle facilitator, an Akashic Record Reader, a trained energy healer, a 200-hour yoga teacher, and an author.

@farahorths

www.farahorths.com

We hope you enjoyed this Hay House book. If you'd like to receive our online catalog featuring additional information on Hay House books and products, or if you'd like to find out more about the Hay Foundation, please contact:

Hay House LLC, P.O. Box 5100, Carlsbad, CA 92018-5100
(760) 431-7695 or (800) 654-5126
www.hayhouse.com® • www.hayfoundation.org

———

Published in Australia by:
Hay House Australia Publishing Pty Ltd
18/36 Ralph St., Alexandria NSW 2015
Phone: +61 (02) 9669 4299
www.hayhouse.com.au

Published in the United Kingdom by:
Hay House UK Ltd
1st Floor, Crawford Corner,
91–93 Baker Street, London W1U 6QQ
Phone: +44 (0)20 3927 7290
www.hayhouse.co.uk

Published in India by:
Hay House Publishers (India) Pvt Ltd
Muskaan Complex, Plot No. 3,
B-2, Vasant Kunj, New Delhi 110 070
Phone: +91 11 41761620
www.hayhouse.co.in

———

Let Your Soul Grow

Experience life-changing transformation—one video
at a time—with guidance from the world's leading experts.

www.healyourlifeplus.com

CONNECT WITH
HAY HOUSE
ONLINE

🌐 hayhouse.co.uk   **f** @hayhouse

📷 @hayhouseuk   🦋 @hayhouseuk.bsky.social

♪ @hayhouseuk   ▶ @HayHousePresents

'The gateways to wisdom and knowledge are always open.'

Louise Hay